Behind the Picket Fence

The Lies Women Believe

Dawn Pryor

Ark House Press
arkhousepress.com

© 2022 Dawn Pryor

All rights reserved. Apart from any fair dealing for the purpose of study, research, criticism, or review, as permitted under the Copyright Act, no part may be reproduced by any process without written permission.

Unless otherwise stated, all Scriptures are taken from the New International Translation (Holy Bible. Copyright© 1996, 2004, 2007, 2013 by Tyndale House Foundation. Used by permission of Tyndale House Publishers Inc., Carol Stream, Illinois 60188. All rights reserved.)

Some names and identifying details have been changed to protect the privacy of individuals.

Cataloguing in Publication Data:
Title: Behind The Picket Fence
ISBN: 978-0-6454926-4-4 (pbk)
Subjects: Christian Living; Women;
Other Authors/Contributors: Pryor, Dawn;

Design by initiateagency.com

ENDORSEMENT

I'VE LONG BEEN A fan of Dawn's work.

For the many years I have had the privilege of knowing Dawn personally, I can attest to her generous spirit in both words of encouragement and the practical ways in which she invests into the lives of others. The wisdom of her words, written from the heart, speaking life into the heart of women, are a soothing balm to the soul. Dawn has personally walked alongside me in some of the darkest valleys in my life. I have been the recipient of her prayers, words of encouragement and tangible expressions of Jesus' love for us in the midst of storms that life can bring us.

Dawn is a living example of what it means to be the hands and feet of Jesus. Her investment into the lives of other women, encouraging them to hold on to the love God has for us, is insurmountable. If you have the privilege of being encouraged by her words, you will be blessed and encouraged.

Sharon Witt
Educator & Speaker
Author of 'This One Life, Teen Talk series, and Girlwise & Wiseguys series'

This book is dedicated to all the gorgeous women in my life.
My friends, my family, my chosen sisters.
The girls that walk with me through the good and the bad times, the ones who cry with me and pray for me, the ones who strengthen me and lead me closer to God.
Each of you women are precious and loved more than you could know.

Forever your friend
Dawn xx

CONTENTS

1.	THE DREAM LIFE	1
2.	THE MASKS WE WEAR	6
3.	IT'S NOT FAIR	11
4.	THE PROVERBS 31 WOMAN	16
5.	THE GIRL IN THE MIRROR	21
6.	SELF TALK	27
7.	PERSPECTIVE	32
8.	BE TRUE TO YOU	38
9.	GOD DOESN'T MAKE FAILURES	43
10.	OUR MENTAL HEALTH	48
11.	COMPARING PAIN	53
12.	MARRIAGE	59
13.	MOTHERHOOD	65
14.	TODDLERS TO TEENAGERS	70
15.	BODY IMAGE	75
16.	DISAPPOINTMENT	81
17.	IMAGINATION	86
18.	BUILD EACH OTHER UP	91
19.	FRIENDS	96
20.	THE INNER VOICE	101
21.	THE ME I SEE	106

22.	OVERLOOKED	111
23.	EL-ROI – 'THE GOD WHO SEES ME'	116
24.	LEADERSHIP	121
25.	WOMEN AND HORMONES	126
26.	THE WORDS WE USE	132
27.	OFFENSE	138
28.	WHO ARE YOU?	143
29.	BE REAL	148
30.	MOTHERS AND DAUGHTERS	153
31.	DECISIONS	158
32.	SOCIAL MEDIA	163
33.	SOCIAL STANDING	169
34.	DISNEY PRINCESSES	175

LIFE BEHIND THE PICKET FENCE

For many of us girls we grew up believing in Disney Princesses, castles, and the one true love of our Prince Charming.

We had a dream of how our lives would look, the picture-perfect house with the white picket fence, a loving family with a husband and children. We would have wonderful friends, a great career, and everything else that went with the ideal life.

But like all dreams, sometimes they are very different to reality, and there are times when we are faced with unmet expectations, and we can lose sight of who we are, and who God created us to be.

During those times we can find ourselves looking at everyone around us and wondering where we went wrong, we wonder why God is blessing everyone else, but not us. We become dissatisfied with who we've become and where we are in life, and we start wishing we were somebody else.

If this is you, then welcome to the club. We have all been there, many of us are still there. It is a place where the grass is greener on the other side of the freshly painted fence, where life is good and free from problems. It is the place that we would all rather be.

However, no matter how good things may look, nothing is ever what it seems. There is no such thing as a life free of problems, and the grass is no greener somewhere else.

As you read through the pages in this book, I pray that you would allow God to open your eyes to all that He has blessed you with, and that you would cherish the life He has given you. Don't wish you were someone else but be who God has called you to be. Live out your purpose in the place that God has planted you, and let all that you are, bring glory to Him.

1

THE DREAM LIFE

BEHIND THE PICKET FENCE is the life we all want.

It's a life that's easy, it's filled with perfect looks, perfect relationships, and perfect people.

As little girls, in one way or another, we all dreamt of this. We all thought that one day we would grow up, move out from our parent's shadow, and live the life we were called to.

We dreamt that we would do things differently, that our lives would somehow be more meaningful, our careers would bring us more success, and the families we would grow would somehow be better than the ones we came from.

We look at our friends and think I will have everything they have and more. I will have the Prince Charming, the Von Trapp children, the cute fluffy dog, and of course, still be able to hold down the fulfilling and successful career.

In our dreams about life, we truly believe that we can and will have it all.

Sadly, we wake up from that dream at some point, and reality hits us with the force of a speeding train. No matter how hard we work at that perfect life, we are never able to reach it. Certainly not from our lack of trying, but more truthfully because there is no such thing. There is no perfect life. The picket fence theory is not reality, it's a myth that we grew up believing. Just like the fairy tales we all read as little girls, the stories of 'living happily ever after' don't always work out like we think they might. We are not always going to be Cinderella or Sleeping Beauty. Sometimes our prince won't come, we won't be swept off our feet, or awoken from our sleep by the kiss of our one true love. No matter how much we want a happy ending, sometimes reality is nothing like the story we read.

I too dreamt of the beautiful home behind the white picket fence. The homes on Wisteria Lane from the popular television series 'Desperate Housewives', the Hamptons lifestyle. I believed that everything would always look pristine, that if I could live in a house that looked that beautiful, then of course, my life would be perfect.

I never stopped to think about the cost involved in owning a house like that, the expenses in running this home, the mortgage, the upkeep. The fact that my Prince Charming would need to work two, or even three jobs to keep us in the way I wanted to become accustomed. Not once did I think about the mess a puppy and then eventually children, would make in this home. It was nothing like how it looked on tv, the image I wanted to portray was side swiped by the truth of life.

The picket fence moved from being the dream to being the downfall.

For each of us there have been dreams that we have held onto all our lives; hopes, thoughts, plans and prayers that we have wanted so badly that we would go to any expense to have.

We see the lives of others around us, friends, family and colleagues and we think 'If only my life looked like that, I would be happy'. We suddenly lose all perspective and find ourselves in a place of comparison.

We see the girl who lives in the beautiful house behind the fence, and we think she has it all, yet we have no idea of what she is sacrificing to live there, we have no idea if she is happy, we don't know if her marriage is rock solid, or her faith is strong. All we see is that she appears to have everything we always wanted, and she is living the life we can only dream of.

This is the kind of thinking that can inadvertently ruin our lives, because we lose sight of all that God has given us, all that He has planned or purposed for us, and we become caught up in coveting something that is not from Him and is not for us.

The fairy tales we've read, the movies we've watched, the dream that has run through our own minds on repeat year after year, have seen us searching for something, waiting for something, and sometimes sacrificing everything, and yet they may never become our truth.

There is a plan for each one of us that is special. It is not a carbon copy of what your friend or sister has, but it is unique to you and I. God did not make us clones of one another, He made you to be special in your own way, and He made me to be special in my own way. We have different giftings, different personalities, different strengths, and different weaknesses. Although we may dream some of the same dreams, for each of us there will be different outcomes.

There is no point in you wishing you were me, living the life I am living, and vice versa, there is no point or benefit in me wishing I was you. In fact, the more we try to be like each other, or to have what the other has, the more we are saying to God that we are not satisfied with the job He has done, or what He has given us.

Hebrews 13:5 (BLT) says
'Let your manner of life be without covetousness, being satisfied with the present'.

There is so much in this verse that we could and should draw on. If we were content within ourselves, we would not be wishing we were someone else, we would not be looking for more, but we would be happy with what we have. We would not be striving, but we would be resting.

True contentment has no place in the world of comparison, in fact they are the total opposite of each other. If we are busy comparing ourselves with those around us, how can we possibly be content. How can we live our lives in peace, when we are filled with the turmoil of wanting more?

I would encourage you today, before you move on to the rest of this book, to think about the life you are currently living, think about how you feel about your life. There is nothing wrong with wanting to do better, or aiming to move out of poverty, or despair. There is nothing wrong with building your career or becoming successful. There is certainly nothing wrong with having high aspirations or dreams but think about your reasons for wanting them.

Are you desiring more because you've compared your life to someone else, and you've come up wanting? Or are you truly looking to better yourself? There is a vast different between the two.

There is nothing right or good about coveting, and we know that the ten commandments tell us the coveting is a sin.

Deuteronomy 5:21 (NIV) says
'You shall not covet….'

So, today before you move forward, give some thought to why you want what is behind the picket fence. Let God speak into your heart and show you if your desires are from Him, or if they are the dreams of a little girl, that you've never let go of. If you find that in fact you must start letting go, do it today, don't hold onto something that was never meant for you, but let God put fresh dreams in your heart, and while you're waiting, learn to be content and trust Him in the journey.

'Don't let the dream become the downfall'

2

THE MASKS WE WEAR

At some point in our lives, we all wear masks. We wear the mask of happiness, the big painted on smile, the cheery singsong voice, and the glazed over eyes that shine just a little too brightly. We wear the mask of contentment, pretending that all is well in our world, that we are happy with our lot in life, and that we have full and grateful hearts towards our friends, family and current situations. We also wear the mask of Christianity, lest anyone gets to see the real us, and be disappointed. It is better to let them see what we want them to see, the woman who forgives, who loves unconditionally, who turns the other cheek, and whose husband and children 'rise up and call her blessed'.

As women we find it so hard to be real and authentic, we want to be liked, we want the admiration of others, we want to be seen as a role model and as the woman who has it all together.

We struggle with the concept of just letting others love us for who we are, rather than who we want them to think we are. We seem to find it incredibly difficult to just share our warts and all, because surely if they knew us on a deeper level, they might be disgusted, they may choose to walk away from us, or they may even look down at us and find someone new as a best friend.

A lot of our behaviour, or our distorted thoughts, come from our upbringing. Maybe we grew up with a mother who always portrayed that she had the perfect family, when really it couldn't be further from the truth. Maybe our upbringing was like living in the Von Trapp family, where performance was everything and everyone needed to always be prepared to break into song when guests came to visit. Maybe like Homer Simpson, our family motto was, 'Remember as far as anyone knows, we're a nice normal family'.

We could fit into any or all of these scenarios, each family is so different with the way they show themselves off to the world. Nobody wants to be seen as less than, so we put on our mask of choice and present the united face of happiness, confidence, joy and resilience to the world at large.

Everything seems perfect, until it isn't.

The problem with masks is that they can't stay on forever, eventually they slip down or wear out. They lose their elasticity, and at some point, they become soiled by everything that touches them.

We have all known the hardships of mask wearing during Covid. We have felt how uncomfortable they can be, how hard it is to read faces and really interpret what someone might be saying.

Masks are not the solution for day-to-day living, they are simply a cover up, a short-term fix and an unhealthy and toxic environment to be trapped in.

So, why do we do this to ourselves? Why do we put on a coverup and hide who we are? Why do we choose to live our lives without freedom? And mostly, why do we rob not only ourselves, but God, of the opportunity to do something beautiful with who we really are?

Luke 12:2 (MSG) says

'You can't keep your true self hidden forever, before long you'll be exposed. You can't hide behind a religious mask forever; sooner or later the mask will slip and your true face will be known'.

Mask wearing is not something new that is only being practised today. Both men and women have been disguising themselves for hundreds of generations, they have been pretending to be something different to what they really are, and for the most part they have failed. Because life is meant to be lived truthfully, we are meant to share who we really are, we are meant to do community together, and that requires us to be honest and true.

You may be looking at the lives of the women around you and thinking they have it all together and you are floundering, you may think that their lives are the airbrushed version of yours, and that what you see when you look at them is one hundred percent genuine.

You couldn't be further from the truth. Not one single woman you know is showing you the entirely true version of herself. She is not letting you see behind the façade to every inch of her life, and you certainly aren't getting the unedited reel.

When you look at others around you, what you are getting to see is mostly the same thing as you are showing to them, the pretty bits, the fun, the Instagram worthy and the 'I have it all together' mask that we all tend to live behind.

When you look behind your neighbour's picket fence and see how green their grass is, don't be fooled into thinking their whole yard looks like this. Sure, it might look great from the street, but what does the backyard look like? Is it still perfect and flourishing back there where no one can see it? Or is it overgrown with weeds, and riddled with prickles?

What you see isn't always the full story, it's not the bigger picture, it's just the part on show.

We can't keep our true self hidden forever; it will eventually be exposed. Nobody can keep up the pretence of perfection, it just isn't realistic. Our true selves are who we are at the depths of our being, they are our core, and it is our true self that we need to share with others.

Why do we need to be exposed? Why do we need to be vulnerable and show our hearts to those around us? Why do we need to take off our masks and let our friends, our family, our colleagues and our neighbours see the real us?

Because this is how we live authentic lives, this is how we share our stories, how we walk with others and encourage them through their hard times. This is where we give others opportunity to gather around us, to carry us in our dark times, to help us when we can no longer help ourselves.

When we are willing to take off our masks, to let down our wall of defence, and to simply share who we are, we are not only giving ourselves the opportunity of being real, but we are letting the girls around us be real too.

As long as we hide, and we fake it, we are living a lie and underestimating the power of God in our lives.

We are not giving God the chance to move in us and through us, allowing Him to draw others to us, and in return draw us to others. We are staying locked behind our closed doors and protecting ourselves from being seen, and from being loved.

We are teaching our daughters to do the same thing, to pretend that everything is ok and that they've got it all together. Sadly, this shows them that they need to push down who they really are, to squash their hurt and their disappointments, and to show the world that regardless of what is going on around them, they are doing great. We are teaching them to hide who they really are or what they are going through, and to water down everything that is important to them.

For us to move forward, to be honest about our feelings, to share our true selves with others, we need to take off our masks. We need to let others see us just as we are, with our messy hair and even messier lives. We need to share with the younger generation that life can be hard, marriage can be hard, motherhood can be hard, trying to have it all, can be downright hard.

It's time to move out from behind our self-made coverings and show the world who God created us to be. To show off our truth, even if it's not pretty, to open our hearts even if they are wounded, and to share our brokenness even if it comes with ugly crying and unbelievable shame.

The time for hiding is over, be brave and be bold, let your true self be known, and share who you really are.

Be the woman who steps out first, take off your mask and set in motion the opportunity for God to shine in you and through you.

'Take off your mask and allow
God to shine through you'

3

IT'S NOT FAIR

WE ALL GO THROUGH times in life of facing things that aren't fair. We look around at others in our circle, and their life seems to be just perfect, yet we seem to be faced with trial after trial.

It's hard when we are comparing our lives to the lives of others, to see anything that is positive, especially when we are walking through hard times.

Unfortunately, sometimes we do walk through the valley, when there appears to be no good, when all around us is sinking sand and darkness.

Luke 4:18 (ICB) says
'…. God sent me to free those who have been treated unfairly.

Jesus has come to dwell with those who are crying 'it's not fair'. He sees the life you're living, He notices your tears and your disappointments, and He feels your heartbreak and pain. You are not alone.

Sometimes during our moments of despair, it can be easy to think that we're in isolation, to think we're facing our current situation on our own. But I have learnt, and I want you to know my friend, you are never alone, God is always with you.

Whatever you are facing today, it's just for a season. This is not the definition of your entire life, it's just a fleeting moment. So, no matter how much it hurts, how much you think this will last forever, or how sure you are that you are the only person who has ever been through this, it's going to pass.

It's when we walk through these times in our lives, that we struggle the most with how it looks on the other side of the fence. When your sky is grey, it appears that for everyone else it's blue. When you have faced endless job rejections, yet your friend lands her perfect job, when you have prayed without ceasing for a baby to fill your womb, and everyone around you is now holding their children. Life can seem very harsh and unfair, and God can feel so far away.

It's in those moments that it can be so hard not to wish for something different, it can seem almost impossible to believe that our ship will come in, when in the natural it looks like our ship has already sailed, and we've been left behind.

James 1:12 (ESV) says

'Blessed is the man who remains steadfast under trial, for when he has stood the test, he will receive the crown of life, which God has promised to those who love Him'.

This is such a great promise to hold onto when we are faced with what appears to be unfair, or when we are walking through a trial. If we can remain steadfast, if we can keep our eyes on God, we will receive a crown which is His gift to us.

I know that keeping focused on God, rather than on our situation can be hard. It takes so much discipline to not become overwhelmed, to not be looking at those around us, to not give up in believing for something better, but to keep trusting God that He has a great plan for us.

There have been times in my life when I have taken my eyes off God and focused on myself and what I was going through. I have been overwhelmed by negativity and frozen by turmoil. I have doubted that God could intervene because His schedule hadn't looked like mine, and I have taken matters into my own hands. Rather than this helping me, it made a landmine out of the situation. I turned my molehill into a mountain and fixated on everything that was wrong in my life. Instead of believing God for the answer, I kept pounding away for a solution, yet making no headway. All the time that this was going on I was looking at those around me, and the cry of my heart was always the same 'It isn't fair'.

I found that I was fighting with God, and if I kept comparing my issues to those of my friends, those who appeared to have it all together, I was never going to be able to move forward and would therefore always be in an argument with God.

If ever there was a time for someone to call on the 'unfairness' card, it was Jesus on the cross. He was a man without sin, He was the son of God, a spotless lamb who had done no wrong. Yet He finds Himself hanging between two men who were indeed sinners, who had knowingly done the wrong thing. He should never have been there, yet He was. Jesus never compared Himself to them and called out for justice, or for a retrial, or for retribution. Rather, He asked His father to forgive those who were about to kill Him.

There is so much we can learn from this story, we can learn about grace, about forgiveness, about love, about burdens and about the will of God.

So often in our despair we look for a way out, we want a plan B. We cry, we compare, we sulk, and we stomp our feet like children. We don't want to suffer, we don't want to go without, and we most certainly don't want to wait. It's not in our nature to sit back and hope that things will get better, we often feel that we need to be doing something, and that we can only move forward if we are carving out a path for ourselves.

However, God's plan is that we trust Him, that we allow Him to lead us, and that we have faith in Him with all that we are going through. He knows that once we have started comparing our situation to those around us, we are going to give up hope, and we are going to fall.

Can I let you in on a little secret? If you are going through something hard, you can be guaranteed that so is your neighbour. Her hard might be different to yours, it might come with different packaging, or be a different colour, but it's hard all the same. You may be suffering with an illness, hers could be a broken marriage, yours could be prodigal children, hers could be the death of a loved one.

Don't look over the fence and think her shade of green is better than yours, it's just different. Your grass might be longer, but hers might have more prickles.

Each one of us faces moments of thinking life is unfair, of suffering through hard times that we think will completely overwhelm us, and in these times, we can't possibly imagine that anyone else is going through the struggles that we are, but that's not true.

Everyone has a journey that includes valleys as well as mountaintops, just because you can't see where someone else is on their journey doesn't mean it's all good. Just as you don't necessarily let others see what you are going through, it can be just the same for them.

No matter what you are facing, do it with faith. Hold onto God in the midst of your suffering, don't look inwards, don't look outwards, but look up. Keep your eyes on Him, and bring your burdens before Him, knowing that He cares for you.

Remember, life isn't always going to be fair, and it certainly isn't always going to be perfect, but if you can remain steadfast in the trial, He will give you the crown of life, just as He promised He would. Hold on to God in each and every circumstance, knowing that His love for you goes deep and wide, and that through all things, He is with you.

> *'Don't look inwards,*
> *don't look outwards, but always*
> *look upwards towards God'*

4

THE PROVERBS 31 WOMAN

IF EVER THERE WAS a woman that we could compare ourselves too, it's the saint of Proverbs 31.

I learnt early on in my life as a wife and a mother that I was never going to be like her. Firstly, I'm not an early riser, I hit my peak between 10-2, anything other than that can be hit and miss. Secondly, I don't sew, not even darning, whatever needs fixed can just as easily be replaced. Thirdly, cooking isn't really my thing, we need to eat, so I'll whip something up, but it's not a great passion of mine. And lastly, my husband and children are not rising and calling me blessed, certainly they say some nice things to me, but nothing that would compare with how this woman is revered.

So, although we can't compare ourselves to this incredible woman, it should be our aim to endeavour to model ourselves after her. She has some beautiful attributes that we could learn from.

'She is more valuable than rubies' (V10):

What woman wouldn't want to be described as being more valuable than a precious stone? Well, that is how God sees each one of us. To Him we are far more valuable than gold, silver, or any precious stone. We don't need to try to be the Proverbs 31 woman in this regard, for we already are, each of us is of immense value to God.

'She is a good wife to her husband, she brings him comfort and encouragement, she is trustworthy and will endeavour to bring only good to his life' (V12):

This should be the aim of all wives, that we would bring all that is good and comforting and encouraging to our husbands and our marriages. This can be difficult at times, especially in the early days when we are still adjusting to married life, but it is certainly something we should work towards. It takes time, commitment, prayer, and a lot of compromise to get it right, but it is in doing this that we build strong and committed marriages.

'She is the most incredible homemaker; she gets up early to prepare meals for her family. She orders food from near and far, works diligently from early morning to late at night' (V14-17):

For some of you this is easy, you love to cook, you google lots of great recipes, you buy yourself a Thermomix, or a Kitchen Aid, and you whip up nutritious and delicious meals for your family. For the rest of us it's all about packet pasta, pre-made salads, and BBQ's. As for getting up early and staying up late, thankfully this is not written into our vows, and there are no parenting books that say this is a must. God loves you every hour of every day, regardless of what time you're at your best.

'She thinks before she makes decisions. She is careful with her choices, and where she invests her time and her money' (V26):

I think there is a lot for each of us to learn in this aspect of her life. We need to have clear and concise thoughts; we need to give careful attention to the things we do.

It can be easy to jump in and make decisions based on emotion, or to get carried away in the moment, but each of us will need to give an account of where we spent our time, or what we did with all that God has given us. Therefore, we need to make our decisions when we have a clear mind, and we are not tossed around like a boat in the ocean.

'She is charitable, she gives to the poor, she shares from the abundance of all she has' (V20):

This can be easy when we are blessed with much, but when we don't have a lot to spare this can prove more difficult. However, there is a lot we can give that has nothing to do with money. We can teach and mentor the younger women, giving them our time, sharing with them our abundance of knowledge. We can model for them marriage and motherhood, we can care for their children, we can encourage them in their growth, and we can pass on our skills, in whatever area they happen to be.

'She outfits herself, her family and her home in fine linen' (V22):

This one could be my downfall; this amazing woman sews (she probably knits and crochets too). I don't sew, and I can't read a pattern, if it can't be bought, I can't have it. Unfortunately, I can't get around this one, I'm beat here. But I'm not going to put myself down, feel bad about myself, or wish I could be someone else. I accept that there are some areas of life that I just won't excel in, and this is one of them. I'm ok with that, it won't stop my family loving me, and it won't stop God loving me, so I'll just move on.

'Her husband is well known and respected' V23):

Thankfully this isn't something we have any control of. Our husbands are not our responsibility, we don't make them who they are, and we certainly can't make people respect them. All we can do is build them up, love them and ensure that our children honour them. Don't compare your husband to someone else's, you don't know what goes on behind closed doors, he may seem like the most wonderful man in the world, but you don't have to live with him. Love the husband God has given you.

'She is clothed with strength and dignity, and she speaks with wisdom' (V25):

A woman's strength comes from her confidence, she knows who she is, and she is comfortable with this. I think this is one of the most important aspects of this woman. She doesn't need to be someone else; she doesn't falter in being herself. She carries herself with dignity because she is confident in who she has been created to be. She shares her Godly wisdom and teaches with both kindness and conviction. There is a lot to be learnt here, we can know who we are in Christ, and we can walk in His truth, teaching and sharing in love.

'Her husband and children rise up and call her blessed' V28):

Having read all the amazing things about this woman is, she deserves blessings from her family. She sacrifices everything for her them, she loves unconditionally, she goes above and beyond. In thinking of our own family, and of our children, we as mothers would do anything for them, we bend over backwards to ensure they have good lives, the best of everything we can give them. For our husbands, we take care of their every need, we are available to them physically and emotionally. We often hold down jobs outside the home, and we still give our family our all. As a wife and a mother, you too are blessed; you too deserve praise. It may seem that all you do is overlooked, but when you stop doing it, you can be sure that it will be missed. You may not get the thanks that you deserve but know that your Father in Heaven sees all that you do, and as much as you do for the least of these, you do for Him. You are blessed.

'She is a woman who fears the Lord, she knows that her beauty will one day pass, the life she is living will one day slip away, but her relationship with God will outweigh everything' (V30):

This is something for all of us. This moment in time is just that, it's a moment, and like all seasons, it will pass. We need to keep our eyes and our focus on the one who truly matters, on the author and finisher of our faith. This life isn't about what we do or don't have, or what we can or can't do. You and I have different gifts, so the things we achieve will be different, and that's a good thing, that's a reason for celebration. God will never compare us, because He created us all differently, all He requires from us is undivided devotion. Live a life of fear and reverence before God, allow Him to be the reason for all that you do. This my dear friend is the epitome of the Proverbs 31 woman.

> *'A woman's strength comes from her confidence in knowing who she is'*

5

THE GIRL IN THE MIRROR

Girls let me break this bit of information to you, in case you don't already know.

THE MIRROR IS NOT ALWAYS GOING TO BE YOUR FRIEND.

There are some days that you will look in the mirror and you might be pleasantly surprised by what you see, and then there may be other days, possibly lots of other days, when you will look in the mirror and you will not be at all happy. There are too many lines on a face that was once line free, your breasts are no longer where they used to be, and they are most certainly not as perky or luscious as what they once were. Your streamlined, athletic and well-toned body is somewhat askew, and your once vibrant locks appear lifeless and dull.

Yes, my friend, the truth of it is all before you in the mirror, the good, the bad and the ugly.

It's hard, I get it, so what do we do with how we feel about our bodies? How do we escape the comparison game when we've just seen ourselves in all our glory?

Well after we've berated ourselves, had a little cry, huffed and puffed and generally decided that we are not fit to be seen in the outside world, we pick ourselves up and find a little perspective.

Firstly, you're not a teenager, so there is absolutely no chance your body is going to look as good as it did back then. No matter how much exercise you do, or how many diets you go on, there are still likely to be 'wobbly' bits. There may even be dimples on the tops of your legs or on your bum. It's a fact of life, as we get older, our bodies change. If you were blessed with the genes of a Greek Goddess, your physical appearance might not be as bad as I'm suggesting, but for many of us, there are going to be body image issues from the time we hit puberty until we die. It's a fact of life.

I can hear you saying, 'But my friend doesn't have flabby arms that go everywhere when she waves'. No, she may not, but I'm pretty sure there are lots of other things about her body she doesn't like. If she doesn't have a voluptuous figure then you can guarantee she is crying about her lack of backside, or the fact that her tiny knees mean no tight-fitting pants look good on her.

You are not alone in your feelings of disappointment over how your body looks, so there is no point in comparing yourself to someone else. All of us are unhappy at some point with how we look.

Can you just imagine how Eve might have felt once the earth started to become populated? There had only been her and Adam to start with, two young lovers each dressed in loin cloth the size of a tissue. She pranced around all day with her six pack, long flowing hair and had nothing to do but look beautiful. However, that wasn't enough for her, like most women she wanted more. She wanted what wasn't available to her, and once she got it, her dream life ended. Suddenly she was hiding in shame, she was covering up her body, and giving up the freedom she had always known. She gave birth to children who grew up to find wives of their own. Eve was no longer the most beautiful woman on earth, she was no longer young and lean, she was older, and wearing the scars of childbirth, raising a family, working and bearing the full weight of the world on her shoulders. How do you think Eve might have felt?

I can imagine that she was disappointed. She had made life choices that determined a very different existence for her than the one God had planned. She went from loin cloth to sack cloth. She went from a desirable young woman to a mother, then a mother-in-law and finally a grandmother. She was no longer who she had once been, and I'm very sure every time she looked at the younger women around her, she felt every bit her age. When she saw the bodies of her son's wives, she would surely think to herself 'I once looked like that'. Just because Eve was the first woman to live, doesn't mean she escaped the comparison game that we all play. When she ate from the tree of good and evil, she was exposed to all the same issues that you and I go through. Once she was open to one lie from the devil, then she was open to all of them, including the one that says, 'You're not good enough'.

So, my friends, we are all in good company, the mirror on the wall simply tells us everything the devil wants us to believe about ourselves. You're too fat, you're too thin, you have too many wrinkles, your hair lacks lustre, you're not enough.

How long will you go on letting yourself believe this?

It may be true that you could lose a few kilos, and maybe a new haircut wouldn't go astray, but neither of those things determine who you are, or should give you cause to hide yourself away because you think you're not as pretty as the girl next door.

You are beautiful.
You are pleasurable.
You are exceptional
You are chosen.
You are loved.

If God has made you, called you, shaped and fashioned you, then you are more beautiful than you could possibly know. Your beauty may not be on the outside for everyone to see, but then true beauty never is.

1 Peter 3:3-4 (NIV) says 'Your beauty should not come from outward adornment, such as elaborate hairstyles and the wearing of gold jewellery or fine clothes. Rather, it should be that of your inner self, the unfading beauty of a gentle and quiet spirit, which is of great worth in God's sight'.

True beauty in the sight of God, is who you are on the inside. God is not looking at whether you have a tiny figure that looks good in clothes, he's not interested in whether you have the latest haircut, or you're wearing the most fashionable outfits. God is looking at your character, how you treat others, how you behave, how you love.

When you compare the girl you see in the mirror to the girl you see down the street, the girl at the gym, or the supermarket, or dropping her kids off at school, you're in essence telling God that His artwork wasn't enough. His creativity wasn't perfect.

You have been fearfully and wonderfully made in His image. How can you possibly argue with that?

We often take on the physical traits of our parents, so if your mum has those much-coveted childbearing hips, there's every chance that you will have them too. If your dad has a roman nose and sticking out ears, that could be who you see when you look in the mirror. Many of our body shapes are passed down through the generations, and unfortunately, there is no escaping them. God created your parents and grand-parents, and He created you too, warts and all. When you were fashioned in your mother's womb, you were intricately knit together in perfection. God never makes mistakes, He is the perfect craftsman, and you my friend are exquisite in His eyes.

So, when you see the girl in the mirror, love her, embrace her, smother her with affection. Don't compare what you see in front of you to what you see around you. You are a stunner! Yes you, the girl with the curvy hips, the big smile, with the happy lines all over her face, you are perfect just the way you are.

As women we need to celebrate our differences, not compare them. We need to raise each other up, to exhort, to encourage and to champion. We need to teach our daughters, our nieces, our granddaughters to love who God created them to be, to not see the flaws in the mirror, but to see the beauty of who we really are.

Gorgeous woman of God, walk away from the mirror knowing the truth of who you are, you are the image of God. Live that out.

'In your mother's womb you were intricately knit together in perfection'

6

SELF TALK

THE WAY WE TALK to ourselves is just as important as the way we talk to other people. Yet it seems we don't take that seriously, we don't seem to have any issues with putting ourselves down, laughing at ourselves, or finding fault with who we are.

Rather than speaking to ourselves kindly, and with love, we use derogatory words and belittling terms. We pick on the way we look, our lack of education, our struggles with technology and everything else in-between. If we can find a reason to put ourselves down, we do.

We put labels on ourselves that even our enemies might not, we class ourselves according to our views on what would be considered perfect. We will look at our friends and measure ourselves accordingly. If they are successful in a particular area, we see ourselves as having failed, if they have well behaved and well-rounded children, we see our parenting as less than, if they have received a promotion at work and we're still pedalling along, we feel left behind and a poor second.

These are lies from the devil, they are to knock us down and leave us feeling like we can't possibly amount to anything. It is his plan that if he can get us to feel bad about ourselves, that if we can talk to ourselves in a negative way, then he is winning in the battle to take over our minds and leave us diminished and broken.

The enemy will at no time give up in his fight to wear us down. He won't stop for one minute trying to make us feel useless and defeated.

We can't let him win, we can't give in and allow him to drag us down into his filthy pit of despair. We need to rise up and believe the truth about who Jesus says we are, as women we need to hold onto His declarations over us and walk in that.

Psalm 18:32 (NIV) says
'It is God who arms me with strength and keeps my way secure'.

If we were to wear labels, two of them should say that we are strong, and that our future is secure. God has given us His strength, His power, and His force, that we might make our way in the world. God doesn't expect us to hide away, to keep ourselves out of sight, but He has strengthened us so that we can walk in freedom, and take on whatever comes our way, knowing that in Him we can have the victory.

With this too, we know that our way is secure, we are surrounded, God goes before us, He walks beside us, and He is always behind us, keeping us safe and leading us into all that He has for us.

So, if this is all truth why do we not believe it?

Why do we walk with our heads downs and our shoulders rounded?

Why aren't we standing tall in the knowledge that we are daughters of the king, we are heirs of the throne, and we are the descendants of the Lion of Judah?

Many of us are living a life of discontent, a life of wishing for more, or even for different. We are so busy comparing ourselves to each other that there is no possible way of being happy with who we are and what we have. We want the next best thing, we want what someone else has, we want the latest gadgets and the newest fad.

All this wanting leaves us empty inside, it leaves us feeling like we don't make the grade, and that we have missed the mark. We are never going to be truly satisfied if we keep striving for more and more and more.

Each time there is something that we want, something that someone else has, we go to great lengths to get it for ourselves, and if that fails, we begin to inwardly seethe, to be disappointed in our efforts, and to feel like we have failed. This will take us on a downward spiral of negativity, it will lead us to feel hopeless and deflated.

Our problem is not that we don't have, but rather how we react to what we don't have. Instead of seeing the glass half full, we are always looking at what is empty. We covet the green grass in our neighbour's yard and fail to see the flowers we have in our own yard. We find fault in all that we do when we compare it to that of the women around us. Instead of choosing to see through rose-coloured glasses, we allow our vision to become clouded and all we see is dim and faded.

Ladies, see yourself through the eyes of God. He sees you as beautiful, as created in His image, as redeemed, as bought with a price, as His daughter, and as victorious.

To Him you are the world, it doesn't matter what you do or don't have, what you can or can't do, He loves you regardless.

We need to take off the labels we have given ourselves, we need to stop talking to ourselves with words of condemnation and we need to speak over ourselves with words of love, of hope, of forgiveness, and of purpose.

Jesus chose you; He went to the cross for you, and He has set a place for you. If you were not worth saving there would have been no reason for Him to die, yet He did, and as He breathed His final breath on the cross, it was you that He thought of.

Jesus made the ultimate sacrifice for you and for I because He thought we were worth it, because He saw something in us that we can't see in ourselves, because He believed that we were special enough to give up His life that we might be able to live ours.

When you look at yourself in the mirror, don't find fault with everything you see, don't put yourself down and call yourself names. You would never walk up to your friend and say, "Hey fatty, you should lose some weight", that would be so unkind and hurtful. So, if you don't do that to a friend, why do it to yourself? Your feelings are just as important as that of your friend, so why in the world would you purposely hurt yourself like that? Sure, maybe you do need to lose a few kilos, but there are other ways to go about being truthful with yourself about weight loss and exercise. Name calling is never the way to do it, not to your friends, or to yourself.

The same goes with your parenting, or your career, or your marriage, or your homemaking skills. These are all areas where we can grow and develop, nobody has it all together in every area of life, there is always room for improvement, but that doesn't mean putting yourself down. It doesn't give you permission to berate or belittle yourself. If you know you have work to do, then do the work, put in the hard yards, and make the necessary changes, then be proud of yourself. It's not easy trying to upskill, or to admit that you need help, or even to begin to revaluate your life and start implementing some new ideas. It can be daunting when you realise the amount of effort that it will take to turn things around, but in the end, you know it will be so worth it. If you are doing this, give yourself a clap on the back, stand a little taller, and walk with your head held high. You are doing great, you are trying to better yourself, and you are finding your way.

Practise talking to yourself the way you would to those you love, be encouraging, offer words of praise, and find ways to celebrate the wins. Just because you may not have done so well in the past doesn't mean you won't in the future, don't be defined by all that has happened to you previously, but see today as a new day, the day you get to try again and this time you get it right.

Take your eyes off all the other women you know and keep them focused on God, knowing that His truth will lead you and guide you. Don't worry about everyone else in the race, just remember that for you to finish well you need to keep looking straight ahead and stay in the game. It doesn't matter whether you come first, second or third, what matters is that you do your best, and that in the end you are happy with the outcome.

Above all, remember that you are loved, not because of what you have done, but because of what He has done for you.

> *'God sees us as beautiful, as redeemed, and as victorious, to Him we are the world'*

7

PERSPECTIVE

Our perspective on life is the one thing that will cloud our judgement in every area. It doesn't matter what is happening in a situation, the way we think will determine how we behave and the type of attitude that we have.

If we grew up in a home that was always negative, that always saw the glass half empty, or that always thought the worst, then this is going to be the benchmark that we set for all our future dealings with both people and situations.

Sometimes the life we have, and how we live is determined by our attitude rather than by our circumstances. A small-town attitude will never strive for more, it will never expect better, and it will never push the boundaries for something greater. We will stay locked within the four walls of thinking that things can never be any better than they are right now, and that we will never go any further than where we currently are.

God's perspective differs so greatly from ours. He has great plans for us, plans that give us a hope and a future, plans that are not based on what we think, or on what we do, but on His purpose for us.

It has never been God's plan that we stay stuck. He gives us the keys to move into so much more than we could ever imagine. However, God can't do the moving for us, we need to be in a place of readiness, a place where we let go of preconceived ideas, beliefs that hold us back, and perspectives that hold us captive.

One of the greatest things that stop us moving forward is our perspective on how we think life should look.

If you grew up being told that you needed to be married by a certain age, have had children by a certain age, and that you must have forged your way in your career by a certain age, then that will be your perspective of what a successful life looks like.

This can be hugely disappointing for you if this hasn't been your experience. If all those ages have come and gone and you are still trying to find out who you are, where you fit in the world, and discover what the future holds for you.

It can suddenly feel like your life is spiralling out of control if all that you thought was the norm is not your reality.

Our perspective can determine the outcome of all the decisions we make. Our thoughts can lead us to make choices based on certain expectations being met.

I thought I would have a job by now.
I thought I would be married by now.
I thought we would have children by now.

I never thought I would be bringing up these children alone.
I never thought I would be in this kind of trouble.
I never thought this would happen to me.

Every thought we have is a preconceived idea of how we think life will look, what we imagine our future will be, and where we think we are going.

It doesn't generally occur to us that some things will go wrong, that other people won't think like us, or that sometimes bad things happen to good people.

Two people joining together in marriage come into that union with very different ideas, different upbringings, and different perspectives on many things. Although they are madly in love, and they are dreaming and planning a life together, they both have backgrounds that will have shaped them into thinking in a particular way. There will be many years of having to work hard at changing attitudes, behaviours, and thought patterns.

There will be discussions and disagreements about money, about family, about household chores, and about raising children. Both the man and the woman will have strong feelings about how things should be done, this can be based on their own upbringing, and their perspective on that will no doubt determine whether they want to follow in their parent's footsteps or do things very differently.

This can be the same within friendships. Many women struggle to understand each other based on their own thoughts or feelings of a situation. They can only see certain circumstances through their own perspective of it, they can't understand why their friend doesn't see it the same way.

They will go to great lengths to explain their position, to talk it through, to step it out, slowly determined that the other party will eventually see things their way. They cannot possibly understand that just because they think their way is right, doesn't necessarily mean that it is.

Mary and Martha were two sisters who had a very different idea about having Jesus come to visit. Mary saw this as a time to sit with Jesus, to spend time in His presence, to learn from Him and to completely be present in the moment. Martha on the other hand saw this as a time of great excitement, a time where she needed to be rushing around preparing food, organising things, and making sure that everything was perfect for the Messiah's visit.

Two girls brought up in the same house, with all the same values, with the same love and adoration of Jesus, yet they both had vastly different ideas on what it meant to spend time with Him. Both went out of their way for Jesus, yet they did it very differently.

This one act had a huge impact on Martha, she was incredibly flustered and so annoyed at Mary, she couldn't understand how her sister could just leave her with all the work and just sit doing nothing.

I can totally see where Martha was coming from, for I know this is the role I too would be playing, I would be so busy wanting to serve Jesus that I may not actually spend any time with Him.

But we know from this story that Jesus tells Martha that her sister, the one just sitting, the one not helping, the one wasting time, was actually the one who was doing the better thing.

Our perspective isn't always necessarily right, it's not always going to be the best choice, and it won't always be looked upon in a good light. Sometimes we need to look at other options, we need to see the bigger picture, and we need to be ready to accept a thought or an opinion that is different to ours.

Our preconceived ideas on things can ruin relationships, it can ruin ideas, and it can ruin our future. If we are so dogmatic about holding tightly to the way we think things should be, we miss out on what could happen if we just let go a little.

I can sometimes be very regimented, I like to have a plan, and I like that plan to be articulated in a certain way. Sometimes, because I need to stick with the decision that I have made, I miss out on the fun that can be had in being spontaneous. Choosing not to change things up a little, not to be willing to go with the flow, and not to see what happens, stops me from finding out what could be, what the something better looks like, and how it feels to just try something new.

Our perspective can either take us places or it can leave us behind. It can cause us to think that things will never get better, or it can fill us with excitement at what might lie ahead.

If you have always believed that God could never use you, then I guess maybe He never will, not because He can't, but because you won't give Him the opportunity.

If you think the cool girls will never be your friend, then that will probably be your reality, not because they don't like you, but because you will sabotage all chances of friendship.

If you think that you're too old, or too uneducated, or too far gone, then that my friend will be your experience, not because it's true, but because you've set your mind on that and it can't be changed.

Don't let your perspective hold you captive. Learn to let go, to live a little. Give God and others the chance to turn things around for you, to suggest an alternative, to surprise you with options.

PERSPECTIVE

Don't be limited by what you don't know, explore some things, take an interest, change your mindset, and step out in faith.

Who knows, you might just love how things turn out.

'Our perspective can determine the outcome of all the decisions we make'

8

BE TRUE TO YOU

It is so easy in today's day and age to lose yourself, and to be caught up in the hype of being perfect. To put aside who you know you are deep in your heart, in order to be what you think is acceptable or what other people want to see.

Don't be fooled, the best person you can be is you!

God did not create you to be someone else, He did not give you their genes, or ambitions, or ministry, or lifestyle. What He gave you was what He thought was best for you. He designed you for a purpose that only you can fulfil. You are not a carbon copy of your friend or your sister, or another woman that you admire, you are unique, and you have been perfectly tailored to be just who you are.

Genesis 1:27 (NIV) says

'God created mankind in His own image, in the image of God He created them; male and female He created them'.

You and I are not a surprise to God. He doesn't look at us and wonder what happened. He doesn't think to Himself that maybe this piece of art that He has created was a mistake, a designer error, a less than perfect creation. He looks at us with love and with pride. He sees what He formed, and He takes joy in that. He sees every freckle across your face, and He smiles at how He planted them there, He looks at your lines and creases, the ones that cause you grief, and He remembers the tears and the laughter that brought those into being, He looks at the wide hips and He thinks of the babies that were born to you with relative ease due to this amazing contouring. God loves every part of you just the way you are. He never compares you to anyone else, His heart and His love is poured out onto each of us just the way we are.

So, therefore, if we have been 'fearfully and wonderfully made' by Him, why do we continue to try to emulate someone else? Why are we looking over the fence into their yard to see how they are doing life, to watch and to copy their parenting, or marriage, or life skills? God didn't create us to be them; He created us to be exactly who we are.

If God had wanted us to be the women next door, then He could have just as easily made two of us exactly the same, but He didn't. He knew the person you would be when He created you, He knew your needs, He knew the needs of the family He would put you into, and He lovingly created you to fit perfectly into that place.

Many years ago, I watched a tv show called 'Wife Swap'. It was a show where two women swapped lives for a week, each going to live with the other person's husband and children and learning to walk in the shoes of the other woman.

On most occasions this proved to be such a disaster. The woman who came into the family was completely out of her depth, she had no history with these people, she didn't know their likes or dislikes, she didn't usually agree with how they lived as a family, or the rules (or lack thereof) that had been established.

She had to learn how to fit in, how to do things the way the family liked them done, she had to learn new parenting skills and quite often she was at a complete loss as to what was expected of her, as this wasn't the way things were done in her own home.

This is what it would be like for all of us if we were to be someone else. If we try to be our much-coveted neighbour, we would be completely out of sync with our families, they would have no idea what was going on if we suddenly started behaving like someone else, because we thought that other person had it all together or was doing life so much better than us. Our family needs us to be exactly who we were created to be.

God created you to be you, and me to be me. He loves us equally regardless of how different we are, no matter what qualities we may or may not have. We are limiting God if we think He could only love us if we behaved a certain way, or had a certain look, or lived in a certain home. What is important to God is how we live, how we love, and who we are on the inside.

If only we could grasp the concept of how He sees us. God doesn't look at our flaws, our mistakes, or our imperfections. When God looks at us, it is through rose-coloured glasses, seeing only what is beautiful and lovely within us. With all the wrong in our lives, when God sees us, He only sees all that is right.

When I was a new mother, each time I gazed into the face of my beautiful baby, I wasn't focused on the fact that He cried all night, or that He feeds and fusses continually, all I could see was the perfection of that little boy in my arms. As I looked into those beautiful blue eyes of his I was blown away that this tiny little boy belonged to me. He had been created by my husband and I, and he had grown inside me for the last 9 months and now here he was cradled in my arms. I didn't see a single flaw but was overcome by the perfection that he was.

This is how God looks at us, each morning He is filled with wonder in who we are. He isn't waiting for us to do something wrong; He isn't looking for reasons to find fault with us, He isn't comparing us to our brothers and sisters, He is looking at us with pride and hope and love.

So why do we find it so hard to love ourselves?

Maybe you have been told that you weren't wanted, or that you're not as pretty or as clever or as well behaved as your sister.

Maybe you've spent your whole life being the one left out. You weren't part of the group of cool kids at school, or you weren't sporty, so you were never picked for any teams, you lacked the necessary intellect to even be part of the nerdy group.

Somehow you were never enough.

We've all felt like this at one stage or another, that we don't fit in, that we aren't like everybody else, and that we just aren't that special.

So, we start to change who we are to be the person that everyone likes, we join gyms to change our shape, we find careers that make us look important, we buy clothes, jewellery, homes, and cars that we can't afford so that we have what we know everyone else wants.

But somehow in all of this, we lose ourselves. We become less of who God created us to be, and more of a shell of someone else.

In all of this we don't find the happiness that we think we will somehow attain, and we sink deeper into the pit of feeling empty on the inside.

Our true happiness is found in living in freedom, living the life we were called to live, and being the person we were created to be.

Don't waste your time wishing you could be someone else, but make time investing in the real you, grow your skills, share your heart and be the woman God has called you to be.

Learn to love who you are, that is where you will find your freedom, your peace, and your contentment.

'With all that is wrong in our lives, when God looks at us, He only sees all that is right'

9

GOD DOESN'T MAKE FAILURES

As you read through the words on these pages, I want you to remember one thing above all – YOU ARE NOT A FAILURE.

All of us have made mistakes, we've all had moments that were not our finest. We have all done things that we are not proud of, or that have had ramifications that have gone on to cause us problems long after the mistake was made.

Each of us has had days, weeks, months, or maybe even longer, that we would most definitely rather forget.

But every morning is a new start, we are not defined by what happened yesterday, by how we behaved, or by the choices we made that were not ideal. Certainly, we could have done better, but by the grace of God we are given a fresh start to do things differently today.

So, no matter what you think about yourself, whether your heart is heavy or you're beating yourself up about a decision you've made or a thought you've had, nothing that you have done would deem you as a failure in the eyes of God.

He gives us new opportunities to start again, to try a different tactic, to let go of what has already come and gone and to have new beginnings. What we see as failure God sees as a pathway to growth.

Yet as women we hold ourselves accountable with such a high standard of what we think should happen, or believe is right, that when we fail, even slightly, we come down very hard on ourselves.

Believing we are a failure is one of the biggest downfalls we face as women. We are looking around us to see how other women are doing life, and sadly, in comparison we may look like we have failed.

We see women who have amazing figures, and we try to look like them, we diet, we exercise, and we knock ourselves out trying to be a carbon copy of someone else. When this doesn't happen, we feel that maybe we haven't worked out enough, we've still eaten too much, or maybe we should have pushed ourselves harder. We come up with all the reasons why we never reached our goal, and for many of us, those reasons just aren't accurate. We don't stop to consider that due to body shape or bone structure, we may never look like that person, and we need to stop seeing that as a failure, and realise that this is just a part of life

In many instances, fear is at the root of us feeling like a failure. We are so fearful of not measuring up, not reaching a certain standard, not being liked, not being chosen, or simply not being enough.

Deep down we all want to be popular, to have people love us, to be found to be desirable or respected. When all of these things work in our favour, we would consider ourselves successful, we feel like we have made it, and all is well in our small corner of the world. But when this isn't how things work out for us, we are left bitterly disappointed.

We can never determine how someone else will look at us or feel about us. We have no control over the thoughts or actions of someone else. We are not a failure because we were not cared for by someone we loved. We are not a failure because we didn't do well in a job interview, or because we weren't picked for a team.

These things are simply a choice that someone else made that is completely out of our control.

Others will always judge us according to what or how they think, just as we do to others, so our self-esteem or thoughts about ourselves can never be based on the thoughts of others.

When my first born was a toddler I took him each week to the mother's group that we had joined when he was a baby. Most of the children in the group were girls, and the few little boys that we had were very placid and well behaved.

Into that group came my energetic, robust and full of life son. He was never satisfied with doing anything quietly, he liked to live his life on the edge, full of adventure and trying to squeeze as much into his day as he could.

So, whilst all the other mums sat and drank coffee and chatted, their children playing nicely around their feet, I was on a constant lookout, jumping up every two minutes to save the hair of some poor unsuspecting little girl, giving back toys that had been 'borrowed' with force, or whispering fiercely under my breath that certain behaviour was not ok.

In those early years, in those group settings, I certainly felt like a failure. What was I doing wrong that my child couldn't just play quietly with the other children? Was I a bad mother because of how he behaved? I was judging myself as a failure based on the behaviour of someone else. I took situations that were out of my control and judged myself by them.

None of the women in the group told me I was a failure (but there were certainly some raised eyebrows) yet I still felt this way. I looked around me at what I considered perfect parenting and I didn't fit in.

How we see ourselves affects everything we do, how we behave, how we interact, and how we feel about who we are.

The woman who is strong and confident will see the failure of a task as simply a learning curve, as opposed to the woman who will give up when what she has tried has not gone well.

The aim for each of us is to not give up, but to move forward and keep trying. Just because what you tried today didn't work, doesn't mean it won't next week if you try doing it a different way. I'm sure for all the great bakers in the world, not every cake was a success, but they didn't just give up when one of their creation's flopped, they put it aside and started again.

True strength of character is when you get up, get back on the horse, and give it another go.

Isaiah 43:18 (CEV) says
'Forget what happened long ago! Don't think about the past'.

God in His wisdom knows that we will go over and over in our minds all of our failures, He knows that we will keep a reel going of everything that we have done wrong, we will rehash time and time again what we could of or should have done differently.

So, He tells us to forget what happened, let it go, move on, stop thinking about it. I know this is far easier said than done, but this is the only thing we can do in our way towards freedom from what is holding us back.

We will never be able to move or try something new if we are constantly looking back at what we consider our failure. As long as we are holding ourselves accountable based on what we think other people think of us, we are keeping ourselves in a prison of our own making.

It's time to shake off the lies we believe about ourselves, and start believing the truth of what God thinks about us.

We are not failures, regardless of our mistakes or our issues, we are simply godly women who are growing and navigating the world around us. Sometimes we struggle, and sometimes we make bad choices, but this is not what defines us. We are defined by who God says we are, and to Him we are a new creation, we are greatly loved, and we are of immense value. This is the truth that we need to believe.

'Don't give up, move forward and keep trying'

10

OUR MENTAL HEALTH

BEHIND THE WHITE PICKET fence stands a young woman; a mother who has dropped her children off to school, she has kissed her husband goodbye as he has gone off to work, she has cleaned her house and tended her garden. As she stands behind her fence looking into the street, her outward appearance is perfect. She is the epitome of the woman who has it all.

However, as she turns and walks into her home, the daily battle she fights within herself finally wins, and only hours later, with tears in her eyes and a broken spirit, she takes her own life.

She gives in to the soul destroying lies that have been eating her up, she can no longer live with who she is and how she feels, so she resigns herself to the fact that this is the only way out.

She will leave behind those she loves believing this is the best option for them all, that they will be better off without her and somehow, they will move on, and their lives will be richer without her in it.

The family and friends of this beautiful soul are destroyed. How did they not see it coming? Why didn't she ask for help? How could someone who had it all feel that she had nothing to live for?

Her children will wonder if it was their fault, and they will live the rest of their lives believing their mother never loved them enough to stay.

All of those around her will wonder what they could have done to make a difference.

What could they have said? How could they have helped?

We live in a society that has become so fake, so stressed, and so overwhelmed, that there appears to be no way out. We live behind the lies of Instagram and Facebook, we put on nice clothes and pretty smiles, we hang out in beautiful locations, seemingly living the good life, yet inside we are falling apart.

We have become experts at letting those around us only see what we want them to see. We hide the real us behind the big smiles, the endless photos, and the right look.

We would never dream of sharing our broken pieces with our family and friends. They would never understand, they would somehow stop loving us if they knew what we were really like. If they could see into the deep recesses of our hearts and minds, they would be disgusted by who we really are.

So instead, we just keep it all hidden, we cry when no one is looking, we fight our demons on our own, and we spend all our time out in the real world being the woman that we think everyone else will like.

Friends do not let this be your existence. Do not give up on life. Do not hide the truth of who you are, or what you are struggling with behind the ugly and deceitful lie that people will stop talking to you, or unfriend you, or unfollow you.

If you are struggling, reach out.

If you are thinking of ending it, stop and think of how this will affect everyone around you.

If you don't believe that you can keep going, think again.

No matter how bad things may seem, there is always hope.

We as women are all watching each other. We want to see how others are doing life, we try to emulate what others do, or we covet what they have. Yet we don't know the full story. I'm sure many looked at that young woman in her garden and yearned to live her life, and yet she felt that her only chance at true freedom was to take her life.

We can never know what another woman is facing, what she is living with on the inside, how she is coping with all that is going on in her world.

We have no idea what happens behind closed doors. The woman you wish you could be is the same woman who wishes she could just walk away from it all.

Every year, in homes all over the world, families are destroyed by suicide.

According to Australian Institute of Health and Welfare in 2019, 3318 people committed suicide, of that number, 816 were women.

This is unacceptable; this is 816 women who didn't think they could face another day, who couldn't keep going, and who thought that ending their lives was the only option.

This is 816 women who had people who loved them, maybe children, or husbands or parents or friends or siblings. This is women who may have gone about their day looking like they had not a care in the world, who seemed to be living their best lives, and who, according to those around them, had so much to live for.

These women chose to make a decision that was irreversible, they chose to leave behind a legacy of heartbreak, and they chose what they truly believed was the only way out.

Some may say their choices were selfish, others would say it was an illness. Some will understand, and others never will. Some may be able to carry on with their lives after this devastation, others may become stuck and never be able to move forward.

The decision to end a life doesn't just affect the person making the decision, it affects everyone she has ever known.

As women how do we stop this from happening?

How do we make sure that those around us know that they can be themselves with us?

How can we see into the depths of another woman's heart and hold her?

The first thing we can do is live authentic lives ourselves. We can share our own struggles, we can let others see the real us, warts and all.

We can get alongside other women and share the journey with them. We all know what it's like to be on a path that seems to have no end in sight, we know how it feels to be overwhelmed and not know what to do. Each and every one of us knows what it feels like to cry in the night and feel like nobody could every understand.

When we allow our own weaknesses to be shared with others, we are opening up a sacred part of ourselves, we are sharing who we truly are. It's not always easy to let people see the real us, there's always the worry that we will be rejected or looked down on, but there's also the possibility that our weakness is the very thing someone else needs to see so that it helps them move forward in their own lives.

Ladies, let your life be an open book, don't pretend to have it all together. We need to be rocks for each other, to be available to each other, and mostly we need to be praying for each other.

Sadly, the ugliness of suicide is not just outside the church, it is very much inside the church too. Somehow, women, regardless of race or religion, have lost their hope, have lost sight of God, and have found that the only way through their hard times is to end it all.

Find your tribe, build a community, become accountable to others. Look for ways to draw in other women and to love them, to get alongside them and do the hard yards with them.

Don't be fooled by what you see on the outside, but look deeper, remembering that we are all hiding something. That behind the laughter and the frivolous conversation, there is so much more going on.

Finally, don't judge.

If you have never walked in their shoes, you have no idea what they are going through. Some women truly suffer on the inside and that is something we may never understand, no matter how hard we try.

Love as Jesus loved, give and keep giving, and pray without ceasing, this is what all of us can do to make a difference to those around us.

The greatest gift you can give to someone else is to walk with them through the hard times, sharing your life with them, and letting them see you for who you really are. In being the hands and feet of Jesus, you may just save another woman from saying goodbye to the world.

> *'Live authentically, be an open book, and share your life with those around you'*

11

COMPARING PAIN

THERE ARE THINGS THAT happen in all our lives that are painful, that threaten to derail us, and that leave us at a complete loss as to how we can move forward.

I know women who have suffered horrendous abuse as children, who have found themselves in relationships that have broken down, who have lost a child before they had the chance to take their first breath, and who have sadly had to walk through illness that has taken away the beauty of life.

For some the soul-destroying pain of these events has been overwhelming, it has left them rocking back and forth in a fetal position, it has led them to contemplate taking the 'easy' way out. It has seen them withdraw from family and friends, unable to keep putting one foot in front of the other.

There are some situations that we will go through that others will never be able to understand, and there are other situations that we will see others suffer through that we could never possibly comprehend ourselves.

It is in these moments, and during these times, that we will often compare our pain to theirs. We will look at their circumstances and evaluate whether it is as hard or as painful as ours.

We may even roll our eyes at them and think they have nothing to cry about, they couldn't possibly understand what true pain or hurt is, they have no idea what it is to suffer.

We will judge them according to our own standards of what real agony is about, and many times they will come up wanting.

It was never God's intention that we would compare ourselves to each other for any reason, but especially not in relation to pain. That we would think we were in a more broken position than someone else, that we would shake our heads and dismiss their heartbreak as trivial or frivolous, when we consider that what we have gone through is so much worse.

Galatians 6:2 (ESV) says
'Carry one another's burdens'.

This scripture doesn't tell us to compare our burdens, for there is no love in comparison, but we are to walk together, carrying, encouraging and praying for one another, and always respecting each other. Holding up the arms of those who are weary, carrying the load for the tired and worn down, and above all else to love abundantly.

When we are doing these things, there is little room left for selfishness, or for being wholly absorbed by our own struggles.

When we are battling certain situations in our lives in can be very hard to see past them, it can be hard to look outside of ourselves and notice what

COMPARING PAIN

is happening with others. We can become 'me' focused, not noticing the hardships of those around us because we are so intent on dealing with what is happening in our own lives.

We wrongly believe that nobody else could possibly be in the dire position that we are, and that our tears are of far more value than that of our neighbour or friend, because our problem is so much worse than theirs.

I remember many years ago going through a very distressing time in my life. I was totally consumed by it, day and night the problem ate me up from the inside out. I couldn't see any light at the end of the tunnel, I couldn't see a brighter horizon, I couldn't see any hope, all I could see was the misery I was suffering through.

I had a friend who I was sharing some of the details of my hardship with. She was kind, she was supportive, and she was always there for me. However, there were times when she tried to tell me that she knew how I felt, that she had a similar issue and that she understood where I was coming from. I was less than gracious in my response to her, for I felt, with all due respect, that she had absolutely no idea. Her life was a walk in the park compared to mine during that season, she had it easy, she had never suffered like I was, and her even considering that her situation was like mine caused me great angst.

I was totally indignant that she would try to compare our pain, that she would think she knew how I felt, and that she would place herself in the same arena as me. I couldn't understand how she could even think that was possible.

However, isn't this what we all do. We look at our lives, we look at the lives of others, and we constantly compare. Our pain is worse, our situation is more dire, our illness is unbearable, our heartbreak is more devastating.

The thought that whatever you're going through, I am going through it too, but worse.

It is one thing to compare our lives to others and wish things were different, but to think that my pain is worse than yours is deplorable.

In the case of illness, there are levels or degrees of suffering. Whilst I might be facing migraines, someone else is facing cancer. While I might be burdened with back pain, someone else is being diagnosed as terminal.

We cannot compare our sickness to that of someone else, and even if two women are walking the same journey of ill health, their mental capacity to cope with that will be very different. Not everyone is strong, or has a support network, or has the finances to get the necessary help, we are all in different places, even if we travel the same path.

The very mention of mental health is a distressing area for many. For some, anxiety can be overwhelming, where others are more able to cope, and have better strategies in place for dealing with hard situations.

In our society, depression is now very much the norm, it is expected that most people will deal with depression at some point in their lives and will require medical intervention to help them through it.

For those of you who have not been in this situation, you will never truly understand the depth of angst that this illness can cause. You will not know how it can drive someone to their knees and leave them breathless, how it will take every bit of strength they have to stay calm, to keep moving and to not give in to the torment that they are faced with.

I would strongly encourage you to champion those who may be suffering through depression, get alongside them and offer support. Don't tell them to 'get over it', don't trivialise their situation, and most certainly do not compare how they are coping with how you may have coped during your moment of sadness. It is not the same thing, and most certainly not helpful.

Another area that is incomparable is the pain that a mother feels over the loss of a child. Whether the child was stillborn, or whether it had its life cut short, the pain is excruciating and is like nothing else that a parent can experience.

The only women who can possibly understand what this is like, is the woman who has been through it. She is the only one who is qualified to say to another mother that she knows how they feel. The rest of us have no idea, we can't pretend to know, and we have no right to say that we understand, for we don't.

It is in these instances that the kindest thing we can do is keep our mouths shout, don't compare some hurt that we may have experienced with this kind of hurt, it's on a whole other level.

Offer support by praying, by loving, by encouraging and by practically serving the family, but don't offend by comparing your pain to theirs.

For each of us, our hurt is real, our feelings are valid, and our emotions can be delicate and raw. We all have journeys that are distressing, that we feel may break us, or pull us into a pit that we can never come back from.

No matter what we are going through, it is no better or worse than what anyone else is going through, and therefore we can't compare situations.

Your background and life experiences are different to mine; therefore, it can be expected that we will react or relate to situations differently. However, regardless of what we are facing, all the things that we go through can have a deep and lasting effect on us.

Your pain is yours and yours alone, and likewise, so is mine. It's not a competition as to who is doing it worse. Let's remember that as we carry one another's burdens.

'Love, pray, encourage and serve — don't compare'

12

MARRIAGE

ANY WOMAN WHO HAS been married for longer than five minutes, knows that it is hard work. It takes a huge amount of dedication, a lot of patience, and great inner strength.

In the lead up to my wedding, my fiancé and I were under enormous pressure. We were building our first home ourselves, whilst trying to save and plan for our big day. Added to that was the fact that we had only known each other for seven months when we got engaged, and in that time, I had lived overseas for five of those months, serving God in a refugee camp in Thailand. We were like two strangers who had met, fallen in love, and pledged ourselves to a life together when we had no idea how that would look.

We faced every possible challenge, lack of money, lack of maturity, family issues, and no idea what we were getting ourselves into. On the night of our wedding rehearsal, we weren't even talking. When our Pastor said you can kiss the bride, it was all I could do to contain myself not to scream and walk out.

However, here we are 31 years later, we are still married, we are still in love, and we have certainly grown up along the way.

I had a friend who got married a few weeks before me, her wedding was beautiful, her and her husband appeared deliriously happy, and there didn't seem to be any of the stress leading up to their wedding compared to what we had faced leading up to ours. They were jetting off on their honeymoon, with not a care in the world. They weren't concerned about not having anywhere to live when they got back, they weren't faced with house issues, money issues or family issues. If ever I wanted to live behind someone else's picket fence, it was hers.

Each of us as women face times when we look at others and are confronted with what appears to be perfection, complete harmony, and the total opposite of what we are currently walking through.

As a future bride I was living in the clouds, I was going to marry my best friend and the love of my life, and then I woke up and found myself with a huge dose of reality. The idea of getting married is a lot easier than the actual act itself.

There were arguments over costs, venues, who would be invited, family expectations, and everything else in-between. I started to look at all my friends around me who had walked this road before, and I suddenly realised that I was ill prepared. They all seemed to have breezed through and come out the other side completely unscathed, while I was floundering and feeling totally overwhelmed.

But our wedding all came together, and it was a beautiful day, and something that I will always look back on with such special memories.

MARRIAGE

It is a well-known fact that a wedding doesn't make a marriage. A wedding is just one day, it's a fleeting moment in time, whereas a marriage is a lifelong commitment, it's going the long haul, it's dying to self, and it's an everyday reminder that two have become one.

Mark 10:8 (NIV) says
'And the two will become one flesh, so they are no longer two, but one'.

This means that you and the person you have married, or are marrying, are now physically, emotionally and spiritually joined to each other. This is BIG!!

Once we are joined to someone else, we are no longer in the same place as we were before, there's no such thing as just doing as you please whenever you please, there's no just spending your money on frivolous things the way you did before, it's all about giving and taking, checking in with the other person and making sure that their needs are taken care of as well as your own.

One of the greatest downfalls between friends is when you start comparing your marriage with theirs, when you compare your husband with theirs. This can be very dangerous ground, once you start comparing your husband with the husbands of your friends or family, you can soon become disillusioned and feel let down.

Their husbands may help with the cooking or the cleaning, however, your husband would prefer to be sitting on the couch with his feet up. Their husbands may have powerful jobs and be earning great money, whilst yours is happy just to plod along and is not fussed by earning big dollars. Their husbands may bring them home flowers every week, while yours doesn't see the need for that.

Take my advice, don't do it, don't go there.

Behind closed doors their husband could be someone you couldn't live with; he could be hurtful or deceitful. Not everything that glistens is a precious stone, sometimes a cubic zirconia tries to pass itself off as a diamond, but when the shine wears off, it's not as perfect as you once thought.

Love the husband that God gave you, work on the marriage that you committed to, and stay the course with the best friend who stood before you when you said, "I do".

The grass isn't always greener in your neighbour's marriage, they may have all the same issues as you, however theirs might be hidden a little better, or could be disguised in a different way, but the problems are still there.

Don't look across the road and see something that isn't there, don't fantasise about perfection when there is no such thing, and don't compare your marriage or your husband to that of those around you.

Proverbs 5:8 (GNT) says

'So be happy with your wife and find your joy with the woman you married'.

We can easily translate that to 'Be happy with your husband and find your joy with the man you married'.

For the sake of your happiness, your health and the commitment you have made to your husband and marriage, don't compare what you have to someone else. Don't wish you were living a different life, in a different place with a different person, but love what you have and the life you are making together.

Marriage is hard, but it's also beautiful. It's a gift, the opportunity of sharing who you are with someone else, bringing out the best in them, while becoming the better version of yourself.

Stay inside your own picket fence, passionately keep your marriage alive, and don't covet what your neighbour has. Be grateful for all that God has given you.

Certainly, it can be difficult, there are times when you look at the person next to you in the bed and you wonder how you can possibly continue to love this man, you ponder over how you have drifted apart, you stare at him and find it hard to believe that this is the same person you committed to love for the rest of your life.

It is not easy to stay 'in love', but we need to remain steadfast in our choice that we will love and be intimately connected to our spouse. That we will stick with them through thick and thin, in sickness and in health, and that we will remain married to them for the rest of our lives.

I know there are times when this is just not possible. When there is infidelity or abuse, staying together may no longer be an option.

But if this is not the case, then love and honour the man that God has given to you.

Fight for your marriage when the days are hard, keep the fire burning, resist the temptation to walk away, or to give up, but stick together through the good and the bad.

Hold tight to the promise of forever, cherish the vows that you made to each other, and continue to find new ways of saying 'I love you'.

Marriage can be such a blessing. There are days, no doubt, that you will struggle to believe this, but know that I speak the truth. There are many who wish they could walk in your shoes, so treasure your husband and the life you have created together and enjoy the path that you've walked since the two have become one.

'Be happy with your husband, finding joy with the man you married'

13

MOTHERHOOD

God made each of us unique, so why is it that us mothers are always comparing ourselves to others? We don't have the same gifting's, or talents, or genetic makeup, yet we look at how our friends or colleagues are mothering and suddenly start to feel flawed in so many areas.

I have always been one of those organised, or rather, regimented, mothers. I like order and structure, there needs to be a purpose in what we are doing. I was never the mum who encouraged painting or play dough, those kinds of things made a mess, and there was no room in my life for more mess or chaos. Needless to say, I don't have creative children. But I had wonderful friends who delved straight into those kinds of activities, they would spend hours with their children nurturing their artistic gifts, all the while the housework built up and dinner wasn't made. I would look at these beautiful women and think to myself that I should be more like them, but then I would panic about all the things that wouldn't get done if I dropped everything to create a bigger mess in the living room, so rather than get out of my comfort zone, I chose other activities, like reading books together instead. As much as I admired these mums, I also knew that their personalities were very different to mine, I couldn't be them and they couldn't be me. That just wasn't the way God made us.

So why do we always compare ourselves to others? What is it that tells us that we aren't doing a good enough job, and we need to change to be more like someone else? Why aren't we happy with the gifts that God placed in us, with the desires He has given us, or the abilities we have been blessed with? If God had wanted me to have creative children, then surely my husband or I would have been creative people, or at the very least, one of their grandparents might have been. And yet I find myself thinking my children may have missed out because I chose to be more structured in my mothering, rather than allowing freedom of expression on an easel.

I am not someone else, and neither are you. We are the women God created us to be, and our children are growing into who God wants them to be, regardless of what they may have missed out on because their mother wasn't wired a particular way. The sooner we accept who we are, and stop comparing ourselves to someone else, or trying to be someone else, the happier we will be. Every time we put ourselves down by trying to emulate someone else, we are insulting God, we are quietly telling Him that He didn't do a great job in creating us, and that He should have made us a little differently. Let me tell you, God did an amazing job when He made you, and when He made me. He used a different mould for both of us, and out of those moulds He created something beautiful.

Motherhood seems to be one of the greatest areas in life where women are constantly looking at others, and not necessarily to learn and grow, but rather to see where we could be flawed.

When my children were small, I lived in a constant state of chaos, some days the chaos was mild, and on other days it was out of control. When I gave birth to baby number two, I already had a very active and strong-willed toddler. I'm not sure what I was thinking having a second child when I had barely had any idea what I was doing with my first, but clearly God had a plan in mind, and I was just there for the journey.

My days were a haze of putting one foot in front of the other, somehow managing to get dressed, and all the while, presenting the most amazing front to the world. Yes, I certainly looked like I had it all together, my children were gorgeous and well dressed, they were clever and for the most part well behaved, but the anxiety levels and stress that I felt was definitely a force to be reckoned with.

For those of you reading this, if you have young children and some of what I have written resonates with you, then I want you to know – this is normal! Being a mother to little ones is hard, it's exhausting, and it can destroy any self-confidence you may have had. No amount of reading books on child rearing can prepare you for the real thing. You can follow everything the book says, but at the end of the day you can still feel like you failed.

Let me tell you why you feel like that, and the reason I know is because I have been there and lived through it. We feel like we have failed because we look at the other mums around us, and they are presenting the same face to the world that we are, but theirs may seem a little more believable.

They'll tell you how wonderful it all is, they are getting a great night's sleep, their little Johnny is just so good, and they can't wait to have baby number two or three. However, they are little ducks in a pond just like you, on the surface they are peaceful and serene, but underneath their little feet are paddling like crazy just to stay afloat.

Girls, we are all the same, we all face similar issues. If you are raising children, then you are in the thick of the trenches. You are bringing up the next generation, you are guiding the next Esther, or Joseph, you are raising up a child of promise, you are mothering the boys and girls of tomorrow who will be leaders in their community and amongst their peers.

Don't put yourself down for finding it hard, don't beat yourself up because you struggle with doing it all right. Besides Mary, the mother of Jesus, I don't think there's one other mother from the beginning of time right through to today who has done everything perfectly. We have all had difficulties with our children, with being good mothers, of not finding fault in every little thing we have done.

Sometimes even the best mums can come undone by the antics of their children. How many times have you seen a young mum in the supermarket wish the floor would swallow her up when her toddler throws a wild tantrum? It's humiliating, its soul destroying, and it can completely un-nerve you. These poor young women have done nothing wrong, yet they can feel that their mothering is now being judged and under terrible scrutiny.

As a mum and woman who has been there, take my advice, keep your eyes on God. Don't look at the other women around you and judge yourself by how they appear to be doing, don't be fooled by thinking that they have it all together and you are the only one who seems to be doing it tough.

You are the perfect mother for your children. You may fall in some areas; you may be a bit more regimented or structured, or you may be covered in paint or play dough, but God has given you the children you have, and He has given them the mother they have. Your home life is unique to your family. How you mother is not necessarily the same as your neighbour, your sister or your friend, you are different to them, so you will have your own style. That isn't a negative, that is you living out your God given personality.

You have been blessed with all those who are living under your roof, don't spend your time trying to do things the way someone else is doing it, but do it in the way God has called you to, and enjoy those small treasures while they are still small, they are a precious gift to you from God.

*'You are raising up a child of promise,
the leaders of tomorrow'*

14

TODDLERS TO TEENAGERS

P<small>SALM</small> 127 (CEV) <small>SAYS</small>
'Children are a blessing and a gift from the Lord'.

There is nothing like having teenage children to show you just how badly your picket fence looks in comparison to your neighbours'.

I was blessed with beautiful, but incredibly strong-willed children. They are adults now, but when they were young, my life was full of challenges. One child more so, had me living on the edge, teetering between despair and full-blown catastrophe. If ever I was living the comparison game, it was during that particular time in my life.

I had envisioned my life with children to be full of love and that I would enjoy every moment. I had expected that each day I would be filled with gratefulness for the life I was living. I most certainly was not prepared the reality of being a mother, for sleepless nights, (which went on for years) tantrums and tears, and battles that would wear down the most hardened soldier. I hadn't counted on hostility, hatred or desolation. My thoughts of motherhood were nothing like the reality I was living.

When we think of blessings, we only see it in the light of good, but sometimes blessings can come as a challenge. During the years of having teenagers and young adults, I was certainly challenged. I was ill prepared for all that I was dealing with, and some days I doubted that God had blessed me at all. However, all these challenges, or blessings, certainly kept me close to God.

Across the road, comparatively speaking, lived the perfect family. They had nice, easy-going, God fearing, parent respecting children. There was nothing about that family that looked like mine, and I desperately wanted to be them! I cried out to God asking why He couldn't have given me that kind of 'blessing'.

In my inability to cope with what I had, I wanted to live on the other side of the fence. The problem with that is that I lost sight of all the goodness in my own home, and only focused on the negative. I caved into believing the lie that someone else had a better life than I did. In reality, my neighbour was suffering in other ways, yes on the surface her life looked great, but just like me, behind closed doors she had her own set of battles to fight.

Love your children; they are a gift from God to you. They might not be packaged exactly the way you would like them, but then we're not packaged exactly the way God would like us to be. Learn to trust in God during the hard times (and there could be many), offer grace despite everything, and be grateful to God for the reward and heritage He has given you.

I know, it can be difficult to be grateful during the challenging times. It can feel like we are facing an uphill climb, it can appear to us that every other family around us is doing it easy, while we are struggling with immeasurable difficulties.

For some it can definitely be harder than others. I know of families where their teenagers have battled with drug addictions, with pornography, with unplanned pregnancies and with mental illness. None of this is easy, and it is a terrible burden for all involved. In each of these situations I can certainly understand the feelings of despair and wishing for something different. I totally get how you may feel that no one has any idea of what you are suffering, and for just one minute you wish you could be someone else. You would give anything for your teenager to be like those next door or across the street, and there is nothing you would like more than to be living behind someone else's picket fence.

However, no amount of wishing things were different will change anything. In the case of living through difficult circumstances, our greatest weapon and our only hope, is God and prayer. That is the only thing that can change the atmosphere in our homes, and what we are dealing with.

Don't look at the other families around you, don't compare yourself to your pastor or the other people in your church, don't put yourself through the anguish of thinking that if you had done things differently you might be dealing with a different result than what you currently have. Bad fruit can still grow on good and healthy trees. Great parents still manage to have wayward children. Not everything is your fault, sometimes even when you have done your best, it still may not work out the way you thought it would.

The first two sons of Adam and Eve were Cain and Abel. Both these boys were raised in the same home and in the same way, yet they both turned out very differently. They were so different in fact that one killed the other in a violent act of rage. Can you imagine how Eve felt about this? She had done all she could do for both her boys, she had loved them deeply, she had given them the very best she could, yet one had gone astray and had taken the life of the other. Through no fault of her own, her son had made a choice that she would have to live with for the rest of her life.

How your children turn out is not necessarily a reflection on you. Sometimes no matter what you do, things can still go pear shape. Even the Godliest of parents can still suffer with heartbreak over the decisions that their children make. Whether you raise two or ten children, as long as there is free will in the world, then there will always be opportunity for prodigals to go wild.

I have some beautiful friends who have raised amazing daughters. These girls to me are the epitome of God-fearing young women. They have incredibly strong values; they honour God with all they are, they serve in the church, and they are true role-models to those around them.

As much as I love and admire this family, they have always been the benchmark that I could never quite achieve. They were my picket fence, the family I coveted, the life I could never attain. These friends were never the problem, I was. I wanted something different to what I had; I wanted their experience because it was easier, in my eyes, to mine. While I was busy looking at how perfect their lives were, I overlooked all that they were struggling with. I was so wrapped up in thinking their family life was a piece of cake, that I never saw that they too were dealing with things that caused them heartbreak, my eyes were closed to any problems they may have had, as I had them on the pedestal of perfection.

God doesn't want us comparing our family to the one next door. He wants us to put our attention into what He has given us, not what He has given someone else. If we are walking through hard times with our children, then He wants us to come to Him, He doesn't want us spending our time looking at others, He wants us to spend our time looking at Him.

If you find this to be your story, my advice is the same for grown children as it is for small children, keep your eyes on God. Looking at those around you and comparing your lives is only going to pull you further into a pit of despair. It is going to cause you undue stress and steal any fragment of peace you may still have. In moments of heartache, whether they are short lived, or go on for years, focus on God, let Him remind you of your worth, and of His great love for both you and your children.

Those who He has put in your care, truly are His blessing to you.

'Sometimes blessings can come as a challenge, these are the ones that keep you close to God'

15

BODY IMAGE

SOMETIMES WE CAN FIND it hard to love ourselves. We struggle with looking at ourselves in the mirror without finding fault or focusing on the negative. We see the slightest flaw and it can be overwhelming. We see that one tiny defect and suddenly that's all we see.

I was born with a port wine birthmark on my shoulder and arm. It is quite large and becomes very red and inflamed when I am hot, under stress or out in the sun. For so long it caused me great angst, it was the first thing I saw when I looked in the mirror, or at photos. I would look at other women's shoulders and wish mine were 'normal' like theirs.

I had many discussions with God over what exactly He was thinking when He created me, and why I wasn't perfect like everyone else.

I hated this one thing about myself, it was my greatest flaw. I tried covering it up with makeup, I tried laser treatment, I tried hiding one side of my body from everyone I met.

It took me a long time to realise that most people didn't notice my birthmark, and for those who did, it was only initially and not really a big deal. It was only in my mind that it was the size of a mountain, the one thing that others focused on, when that couldn't be farther from the truth.

There are so many reasons that women find fault with who they are or how they look. Many grow up in homes where they haven't been valued or loved, others have been victims of abuse that has brought about feelings of shame or disgust. Sadly, we don't look at ourselves the way that God looks at us, and therefore we are constantly disappointed.

There comes a time in every woman's life when she needs to let go of all that she isn't and learn to love all that she is. We need to become our own best friend, the one who will get behind us and catapult us into believing that we are amazing.

There will always be things we don't like about our looks, and there will be some things we can't change, but the one thing we most certainly can change is our attitude, and this is something we need to work on.

So, for just a moment let's talk about that one subject that will make any women weak at the knees and feel slightly sick to the stomach.

Yes, you read my mind, you've taken a big breath in, and you're all set, let's talk about shopping for swimwear.

I know, it's cringe worthy, and fills our minds with a visual that we could certainly do without.

If you are like me, the very thought of parading around in our lily-white skin wearing nothing but a small piece of fabric to cover all our bits and pieces, is a horrific thought. Not to mention when the wonderfully helpful salesgirl wants to check if you're doing ok and can she help you with sizes.

Absolutely not!

The last thing we need is someone else helping us decide if we look presentable enough to go out into the world wearing nothing but a fig leaf.

Now, if you are one of the small number of women in the world who looks at herself in the mirror and smiles with confidence at the vision you see there, this chapter might not be for you, but for many of us, when we look in the mirror, a million different thoughts run through our minds, most of which are not pretty.

Like most of us, the woman I see today is very different to the woman I saw thirty years ago. Back then I was young, I hadn't had any children yet, I didn't need to go to excessive lengths to move weight that seemed to just appear out of nowhere after eating a vanilla slice or custard donut. However, back then I had no idea that 30 years into the future I would look back and remember that girl with love, with longing and with wonderful memories.

Who you are today is beautiful, who you are is special and unique. No matter what you might think of yourself, one day you will look back at who you are now and wonder what you ever criticized about yourself.

Every season of our lives bring with it change, and that can be both positive and negative. But we need to embrace ourselves, love who we are, and be at peace with our outward appearance. We need to stop comparing ourselves to every other woman we know, and just face who we are head-on and be okay with that.

I have some gorgeous, amazing, wonderful, waif-like girlfriends. There have been days that I have certainly felt like dropping them as friends. I have looked at myself in comparison to them and thought it might be easier to just find other friends. It may be less daunting to hang out with girls who were more 'regular' in their looks, more like me. There has been so much about them that annoys me, like how their clothes hang perfectly on their bodies, they don't dread change room mirrors, they can buy outfits in store and online without a problem (in all seriousness, who can shop online without reading all the fine print about returning the outfit due to looking nothing like the model in the picture?).

However, these girls aren't the problem, I am.

When we look at other women, we begin to judge. We are, in this instance, not judging them, but we are judging ourselves. We see how great they look, and suddenly we start focusing on all the negatives about ourselves. They have amazing figures, and we are frumpy. They have great hair, and ours is frizzy and out of control. They walk with confidence, and we slouch a little lower, trying to hide who we are.

Let me tell you something, girl you are amazing!

You are beautiful!

You have been created in the image of God.

You were never made to look like someone else, but you were uniquely formed and shaped in your mother's womb, God lovingly pieced you together, and He takes great pride in you as His child.

You might be tall, or short, a size 6 or a size 16, your hair might be curly or straight, whatever you look like, rock it! Love the woman God made you to be.

If you have scars, they are proof of God carrying you through a season, if you have a little extra weight, it shows that you are feasting from the abundance of blessing in your life, if you have a splatter of freckles across your face, it's from enjoying the sun dancing on your skin.

Don't look at the other women in your life, the ones with the perfect bodies and the flawless faces and wish you were them. They too have issues with their body image, they too are comparing themselves to others.

Do you think the super models of this world are entirely happy with how they look? Don't be fooled, they too are comparing themselves to the other beautiful girls that surround them. They are all battling to lose that extra bit of weight, to trim down their thighs, or alter their bone structure so that they can compete in a world that is obsessed with looks.

It is estimated that approximately one million people per year in Australia are diagnosed with an eating disorder.

That is a disturbing amount of people, both men and women, boys and girls, who are so focused on their body, that they will go to any lengths to change how they look.

When they see themselves in the mirror, they are disgusted with the sight before them. It causes them to binge and then to vomit, or to stop eating altogether.

Our media plays a huge role in telling people how they should look, and what is considered pretty or beautiful. However, they are not the only ones at fault. Each of us contribute to the downfall of the women around us by constantly focusing on how we look, and by comparing ourselves, we are all adding to the problem.

So, ladies when you see that cuddly woman in the mirror, parading around in nothing more than a shoestring, and you're wondering how you can take that body out to the world, just go ahead and do it. Grab a sarong, put on a smile, and get out there and enjoy life. Show those around you that true confidence is found, not in how you look, but in who you are.

Who you are is a much loved, greatly cared for, daughter of God. You are a child of the king, a princess, and a woman of worth.

Love who you are, who you have been created to be, and share that woman with the world.

> *Who you are is beautiful; you are special, you are unique, and you are created in the image of God'*

16

DISAPPOINTMENT

WE ALL GO THROUGH periods in our life when we are disappointed. When things happen that are out of our control, and we are left feeling very emotional, overcome by sadness and bewilderment. This can be for a short period of time, or it can be longer lasting. It may leave a sour taste in our mouths, or it could bring us to our knees in complete devastation.

We can be hurt and let down by friends and loved ones, we can miss out on a job that we wanted, we can be betrayed by our life partner, or we can be facing an illness that can change our future. There are so many ways in which we can be disappointed. However, what is more important is how we deal with it and move forward from that.

Unfortunately, some people choose to live in this state of disappointment permanently rather than accept that things do not always work out the way we like and move on.

The problem with disappointment is that it is tied up with expectation. We assume that things will work out a particular way, and when that doesn't happen, we're not sure what to do. We set high expectations for ourselves, of how we think our lives should look, and when it doesn't happen how we think it should, then something within us snaps and we come crashing down. For the young woman who is climbing the corporate ladder, to not reach certain goals by certain times, can have a terrible effect on her self-esteem. For the woman who stands beside her friends as they say, 'I do', while she's waiting for her own prince charming to sweep her off her feet and lead her down the aisle, this can seem too much to bear. For the married woman who month after month continues to get her period when she is wanting desperately to have a baby, the disappointment that overcomes her is heart-breaking. Of course, there is also the disappointment felt by every mother of adult children, waiting for them to call, for them to visit, or for them to show some interest in the woman who birthed and brought them up. We all face disappointment in some way or another, because each of us have expectations, and sometimes, many times, our expectations are not met.

The one thing that we need to realise is that some of the expectations we have in life are just an illusion, not a reality.

Just because I would love to be the next big thing on 'The Voice' certainly doesn't mean I will be. No amount of wanting will make that happen. Firstly, I can't sing, not even a little bit, so there is no point in being disappointed in something that could never possibly happen.

Added to that, dreaming of living the life of the rich and famous is not a possibility when I work part-time in a simple paying job. We must be realistic with our hopes and our expectations, some things are a possibility, and others are just a pipe dream. Just as we choose our battles, we also need to choose what we will and won't be disappointed about. The simple truth, and absolute fact, is that some of our expectations are just not attainable.

What I want you to know, and I mean really know, beyond a shadow of a doubt is that you are not the only one facing disappointment. Do not for one-minute feel you are the only one dealing with unmet expectations. Your best friend is, your neighbour is, and your colleague is. All of us have areas in our lives where we are overwhelmed, we feel let down, or we are struggling with an unresolved issue. Nobody is immune to the thought that life would be better than what it actually is. If you are looking at the woman in the beautiful house across the road from you and thinking that she has everything in life, she could never be disappointed, you couldn't be more wrong. She too is facing the same hurts, worries and concerns as everybody else. It may be that her disappointments are different to yours, but she has them just the same.

Isaiah 49:23 (NIV) says
'…Then you will know that I am the Lord, those who hope in me will not be disappointed'.

This is the greatest truth we can hold onto. It is only when we place our hope, faith and trust in Jesus that we will not be disappointed. He is the only one who can be our constant, who will not let us down. He will never leave us lonely, and He is the only refuge we have in a world that is constantly moving and changing.

It's when we put our trust in Him, and we let go of all else, that we can deal with everything we are faced with. God promises that He will be with us always, not just when He feels like it, not when He isn't working on something else, not until someone better comes along, and not only on His good days. He will be with us every minute of every day.

This brings me to another area of disappointment.

Don't judge God by how you see things. Just because you are disappointed in yourself, doesn't mean that He is disappointed in you. His thoughts about us are incredibly different to ours. He looks at us through His lens of love and grace. Although we may occasionally make mistakes, to Him we are not, and never will be a mistake. The words He speaks over us are beautiful, treasured, precious, jewel, bride and daughter. There is never a moment that He is so disappointed in us or our behaviour that He would turn away in disgust. No matter what you have done, said, or thought, God loves you and you are not a disappointment to Him.

So how do we deal with what has overtaken us?

How do we move forward after we realise that our current situation is out of our control? Where do we go with our disappointment and expectations?

We need to let it all go. Let go of the hurt, the worry, the wounds, and all that we feel has been unmet. We need to throw our hands up in the air, release the pain and frustration, and turn our eyes on Jesus. This, my friend, is the only way to deal with the disappointments of life. There is nothing we can do on our own to 'get over it', somethings are just too hard.

Take to God in prayer all that you are facing, give Him all your disappointments, and allow Him to fill your heavy heart with His love. It's only in releasing pain that you can be filled with promise. It's only when we admit to Him how we feel that He can do something to help us. As long as we keep everything bottled up, try to hide our pain, and live a life that is filled with lies and deception, then God is not able to set us free.

Finally, let go of believing the lie that you are the only one filled with disappointment, because you most certainly are not.

Behind the picket fence we are all struggling with life not being the way we imagined it would be, and the sooner we are honest with ourselves and each other, the easier each of our lives will become.

Live your best life, not in disappointment, but by being authentically you.

When we place our hope, faith, and trust in Jesus we will not be disappointed'

17

IMAGINATION

ALL OF US AT times can have the most vivid imaginations. We can conjure up in our minds all sorts of things that just aren't happening, are not real, are problematic, and that cause us no end of distress.

We tend to read more into a situation than is actually there and allow it to become a mountain in our minds. We start to believe that other people might be talking about us, that our jobs could be in jeopardy, that we are being ostracized in our friendship group, or that we are no longer wanted or needed.

The mind is an incredible place, it is where our battles are fought, and where we experience either victory or defeat. It is where our sanity is attacked, our beliefs are critiqued, and our hope can be rocked.

No wonder the bible gives us many scriptures on the mind, and what happens there. God knew that we would become stuck, that we would fret and worry and overthink situations. He knew that we would find ourselves in places that would destroy our peace and keep us locked in a dark and miserable place.

Our mind will tell us that we aren't special, that we aren't pretty, that we aren't loved and that everybody else is living a better life than us. It will lie to us, deceive us and have us tied in knots. Our mind will ensure that we focus on the negative instead of seeing the many blessings we have in our lives.

When we allow our imaginations to run wild, we suddenly see ourselves in a very different light. Instead of seeing ourselves the way God sees us, we start to see ourselves the way the devil does. We are a push over, we're weak, we're undeserving and we're going nowhere. We then look around us and see how others are living, how God seems to be blessing them, how their lives and ministry are fruitful, their marriages flourishing, and their businesses are going from strength to strength.

Our imagination is a beautiful thing if it is used well. If we dream big dreams, or find ways of encouraging others, or use it to bring hope into a lost world. It is a gift from God, and He is the one who will use it for good rather than allowing it to be used in ways that will bring us down.

When I wrote the children's book 'I could be anything', it required me to use a part of my imagination that I didn't think I would be able to tap into. It meant getting back to basics, thinking like a child and dreaming the dreams of little ones. But God gave me the ideas, He planted within my mind His words and His hopes for small children. He wanted them to know that they could continue to hope for the future, amidst the very trying times of Covid and during a season in life that children were beginning to lose hold of their dreams that there would be a future for them.

God wants us to use our imagination for good, He doesn't want us to be allowing our thoughts to run rampant and be full of endless worries and concerns. He doesn't want us looking at the people around us and thinking that they have so much more than us, while we have nothing.

Think back to when you were at school. You walk into a room of girls whispering, they look over at you and the next thing you know you are convinced they are talking about you, especially when the hushed tones stop very quickly, and they avert their eyes in a very guilty fashion.

You know without a shadow of a doubt that you were the subject of their conversation, after all, what else could they be talking about?

We have all been there, we have all let our imaginations get the better of us and have thought that all eyes were on us, condemning our behaviour, or judging our actions.

The fact that the conversation could have very easily been about something or someone else doesn't cross our mind, nothing will assure us that we were not the reason for the whispers.

This is the perfect example of letting our imagination carry us away, of believing something that may have a much simpler explanation, and of allowing our thoughts to take us to places that we didn't need to go.

Instead of exploring all the options we home in on just that one thing, that one negative thought that will steal our peace and our joy and will lead us down the path of misery.

IMAGINATION

We read in Isaiah 26:3 (NIV)
'You will keep in perfect peace those whose minds are steadfast because they trust in you'.

To ensure that we keep our peace, we need to have our trust firmly placed in God, and to have minds that are steadfast, not tossed and turned like the waves of the sea.

We need to remain unwavering in our thinking, not be tormented by everything that comes our way, not imagining the worst in every circumstance, and not constantly rehashing every situation we find ourselves in.

In the heart of every woman is the desire to fit in, we don't want to be too different to everyone else. Certainly, we want to be unique, we want to have gifts and talents that set us apart from everyone else, but we don't want to be seen as that different that we are considered weird. We don't want to be the talk of the tearoom, or the class, or the family. We want to be special, but not that kind of special.

However, sometimes that is exactly how we see ourselves, we feel that we are out of kilter with all the other girls in our village, so therefore there must be something wrong with us, and no doubt they are all talking about us. We allow our imagination to totally take over and blow each and every situation way out of proportion.

One sideways glance and we are sure that we are today's hot topic of conversation, that every bit of gossip will be about us, and that our lives will somehow be ruined because of it.

We imagine that we will never make the 'A' team, we will be excluded, as will our husbands and children, because of that one thing we may, or may not, have done. We will be like lepers who nobody wants near them, people will walk the other way when we walk in the room, and we will believe all of this because of the lies that were planted in our minds, instead of remaining steadfast in the truth.

It's a fact of life that not all of us will be liked by everyone around us, we will at some time all fall short of the expectations that others have of us, that is completely normal.

We can't win every popularity contest, or please all the people all the time, it's just not possible, nor is it normal.

We need to be realistic in our thoughts and not let them control us. We need to let go of the desire of wanting everyone to love us, and just accept that there are some people who will never be in our corner, who won't have our backs and who just aren't the type of people we need in our lives.

When you walk into a crowded room and people look the other way, or start whispering, or stop talking altogether, just move on. If they have a problem with you, that's nothing to do with you, that's on them, so let it go.

Stop worrying about how everyone else perceives you, stop imagining the worst and just continue to be you, in every shape and form.

You weren't created to be one of the crowd, you were created to stand out in the crowd, so do just that.

Shine like the diamond God created you to be and allow Him to use your imagination for His purposes, for all that is good, positive and true.

'Shine like the diamond God created you to be'

18

BUILD EACH OTHER UP

Girls, hear me loud and clear, it is not ok to tear each other down to make ourselves feel better.

We are all doing life as best we can, there are areas that are easier for some of us than they are for others and vice versa. Just because I might be better at something than you, that doesn't give me an excuse to make you look bad or feel bad.

There are plenty of things I'm not great at and many things where I completely fail. I can't sew, or knit, or do crossword puzzles. Goodness knows there are some days I can barely put a meal on the table. I would never be the poster child for the Proverbs 31 woman. However, I have other strengths, and giftings in areas that could be different to you.

1 Thessalonians 5:11 (NIV) says

'Therefore encourage one another and build each other up, just as in fact you are doing'.

As women, we need to encourage each other to be the best version of ourselves that we can be. We can't do that if we are looking for faults or finding ways to undermine each other. Each of us is walking a different journey, we all have different shoes, we are taking different paths, and in that, all of us need someone in our corner cheering us on. We need someone to travel with us, to let us know that we are doing a fantastic job in hard circumstances.

I remember well the years of parenting a difficult teenager. I spent so much time doubting all my decisions, crying over every failed attempt, and wishing things were so different to what they were. It was during these times that I needed someone to reassure me that I was doing ok, that not everything was my fault, contrary to how I felt, and that I wasn't going to ruin my child's life by practicing tough love. The thing that I didn't need was for well-meaning friends to suggest I pray about the behaviour or have them constantly let me know how well their child had turned out because of what they were doing. This is not building someone up, this is hurting them, it's telling them they weren't parenting well or that they had somehow missed the mark of what a good Christian mother looks like.

Building someone up always makes the other person feel valued, listened to, cared for and loved. It might mean keeping your mouth closed when what you have to say can seem negative, it can mean even though you disagree with their point of view you treat them with respect, and it can mean keeping quiet about your own achievements when they will make someone else feel like a failure.

Each of us may look very different on the outside, but on the inside we are all quite similar. We have the same basic needs, we want to be loved, we want to know we are doing ok, and we want to live our lives free from judgement.

We all suffer with insecurities and doubts, but we do our best with what we have, we work towards success and we all want to be able to do this with our heads held high.

My fence might be painted a different colour to yours, but all our fences have places where they are peeling, or where the rot is starting to show. Throwing more paint on the fence may make it look better, but it doesn't solve the underlying problem. So, while you look across at your neighbours' fence and it looks perfect, it just might mean it's had an extra brush of paint to hide what is beneath.

This is the same for each of us, we put on nice clothes, fake smiles and bright lipstick and think we can hide behind that. But inside we are downcast, we are hurting, and we are barely holding on.

If this is happening to you, then you can be quite sure that it is also happening to others. You are not the only one who needs help, who needs cheering on, who needs someone to come along side them to let you know that it will be ok. All of us need that friend who will hug us through the tough days and show us that we are cared for in every situation.

You can be that friend, you can cheer on your girlfriends, your co-workers, your neighbours, and your loved ones. Help them to reach their dreams, to fulfil their potential and to become the women that God has called them to be. If you were to look at those around you, really look at them, not just what they show on the surface, then you will start to see the cracks, you will start to hear everything that they are not saying. This is who you need to be building up, who you need to walk with, to share stories of your own struggles with. Put away your pride of not wanting the real you to be on show and live your life authentically so that others will be encouraged, others will see how you got through trials, and they'll start to have hope for their own situations.

It's when we share the hard moments of our own lives with others, when we let them see our own cracks, when we tell them how God walked with us through difficult times, that we enable other women to be honest about their own struggles. It gives them opportunities to share, to unload and to feel safe in knowing that they are not alone on their journey.

This is what it looks like to be part of a village, women in a tribe, all doing life together. Building each other up, encouraging each other and being an example from one generation to the next. It's when we live like this that we build a strong community of women around us.

One thing that I have noticed amongst women, and it's so disappointing to see, is the fear that if we lift someone else up, it will somehow push us down.

Life isn't a competition between us and all the other females in our lives. Strong women help to grow other strong women, which in turn helps them live full and bountiful lives.

For too long we have bought into the lie that if want to be successful then we need to keep others on the level below us, we can't share our success stories with them for fear of them following our lead and eventually overtaking us.

This is very much part of the Tall Poppy Syndrome, where anyone who has shown some level of achievement is criticised, pulled down or held back.

This is not, and never will be, God's ideal for us as women. He wants us to cheer on those who are following their dreams, who are having success and who are making something good of their lives. He has risen these women up, and it is not our place to tear them down, we are to get behind them and cheer them on, knowing that all they have comes from God.

God has a plan for each of us, and it's a plan that includes hope and a future. It is up to you and I to share that with the women around us, remind them of God's great love for them, show them His principles and walk with them through their trials and triumphs.

Do your best to encourage the girls around you, reach out to them, be honest with them and let them know you're in their corner.

Be the woman who leads by example, who gives strength to those who are weak, be the shoulder to cry on, and the light at the end of the tunnel.

Your journey is not all about you, but it's about the circle of friends around you. Live your life as an open book and be an encouragement to others.

In every way you can, build up the girls around you.

'Build up, encourage, and be an example to the women in your village'

19

FRIENDS

As women, our friendships are incredibly important to us, they are our lifeline, our go to, and one of the most valued relationships we have.

For those of us lucky enough to have girlfriends that we love as sisters, we are truly blessed. To have those women in our lives who we can call anytime day or night and know they would drop everything for us, where we can say or do anything without fear of judgement, and know they have our back in every situation, this is truly a gift from God.

However, there are times in all our lives when we look at our friends through the green eyes of jealousy. We look at the things they have, the families they are surrounded by, or the careers they have carved out, and we truly feel the sting of resentment.

It hurts when we get left behind, when our dreams don't come to pass, when our shelf life looks like expiring. All the things we thought we would share with our friends seem like a distant memory, as they move from strength to strength, and we are stuck where we are.

Proverbs 27:9 (TPT) says
    '.... a sweet friendship refreshes the soul'.

There is nothing more refreshing than time spent in the company of your girlfriends. Whether the time is spent laughing, dancing, praying, or crying, being with your tribe, the women in your life, is so good for your soul. Having that time to step back from all your other responsibilities, be that work, children, relationships, study, whatever else you have going on in your life, just taking some time out with a friend suddenly makes the world seem like a better place.

I grew up moving around a lot, so making friends never came easy. I was always on the outer, not being part of the same memories, not having the same jokes to laugh at, not remembering 'that time when….'. I always had to try harder than everyone else, I had to work at relationships more, I had to give and keep giving. It wasn't until my late teens, when I joined churches with great youth groups, that I was able to just walk into a circle of girls and be myself. Where I didn't have to compete, or be the new girl, but I was just accepted as one of the group. Now that certainly was refreshing for my soul.

The girlfriends that I met all those years ago are still my closest friends today, they are the girls I laugh with, cry with, pray with and rejoice with. There have been many other women who have come into my life since then, some have stayed for just a season, and others are firmly ensconced in my heart and always will be. We have clicked, and they have become a part of my village.

However, even amongst friends there are still elements of longing, or wishing, or desiring that things could be different. I have visited in their homes and suddenly needed to do an entire renovation on mine. I have sat with their families at dinner and compared the behaviour between our children, I have seen them interact with their husbands or parents and felt disappointed with my own lot in life.

It's not just social media that has us critiquing our lives, but it's the women we spend time with, the girls we grew up with, the mums in our mother's group. We are always watching how someone else is doing things, we look on and see how they have it all together. They bake, they clean, they let their children play with play-doh inside, it all seems a bit much when you're comparing yourself to them.

I have the most beautiful friend who is a wonderful cook, she also has a magnificent home, a lovely garden, and she does incredible quilting. It would be so easy for me to look at her and feel inadequate, to wish that I had some of her talents. Add to this her rich mane of hair that I absolutely love, and her tiny framed body. It would be easy for me to be put off having her as a friend, she seemingly has everything. But of course this isn't true, she has her own struggles just like I do, she too looks at other women and sees all that they have and notices all that she does not. It is the same for all of us, we face the same struggles, even with our friends.

We need to celebrate our friendships, we need to cheer on our tribe, be happy for them when they have big or small wins. When we know the struggle that they have gone through to achieve something, be proud of them, let them know you are in their corner, encourage them and keep fighting alongside them.

There is an anonymous saying, 'A true friend is one who believes in you when you have ceased to believe in yourself'.

Be that person, let those around you know that you will believe in them when no one else does, that you will be their strength when they can't keep going.

Don't turn your back on a friend just because she's in a season that is different to yours, but continue to be her champion, loving her through the rough days, and cheering her on through every milestone.

Our besties are the ones who need us, they must know that they can call us in the middle of the night and cry, that we will drive over in our pyjamas and pray them through a meltdown. It is more important than you will ever realise for your girls to know that you love them, you're not judging them, and you will go the distance with them.

I remember when my children were teenagers, and we were having a really rough time with one of them. There was one particular instance that had the potential to shatter everything, and I remember crying to my girlfriends in heartbreak. I had come to the end of my tether, I could barely speak anymore, I had hit rock bottom and I just didn't know what else to do. Those girls prayed for me, they prayed for my child, and they just kept encouraging me and loving me. There was nothing they could do to change the situation in the natural, but they went straight to the source of hope on my behalf. When I didn't even know what to pray anymore, they did it for me.

This ladies, is why we need our friends. This is why God gives us the women we have in our lives. He places us in a family that He has chosen for us, with exactly the right people we will need. He sees ahead to the situations we will face, and He brings those around us that He knows will be invaluable to us.

Proverbs 17:17 (NIV) says

'A friend loves at all times, and a brother is born for adversity'.

Read that first part again – A FRIEND LOVES AT ALL TIMES.

That is powerful, and so full of hope. To be that friend and to have that friend, what an absolute blessing. To know that someone always loves you. Not your parents, or your partner, or even God, but a friend. Another woman who has come alongside you, who will go the extra mile, who will rise up when you can't, who will help to fill your cup, and love you.

We all need to be that woman, we need to examine our own hearts and remove all signs of competitiveness, jealousy, bitterness, and selfishness. We must choose to put aside all our own feelings of inadequacy and stop comparing ourselves to the sisters God has given us. The time has come to just love, to share, to strengthen and to uplift our girlfriends.

Give them reasons to believe in themselves, give them the opportunity to be real and give them what all of us want, acceptance.

As you think about the women in your life, whether they are your flesh and blood family, your spiritual family, or your chosen family, look for ways that you can lighten their load, seek out opportunities to encourage them, help them to be brave, to fight the good fight, and to know without a shadow of a doubt, that they are loved.

Be the friend that you want for yourself.

'The time has come to love, to share, to strengthen and to uplift'

20

THE INNER VOICE

SOMETIMES IT IS VERY difficult to hear the voice of God over our own voice. To hear over the voice within us that screams at us throughout the day that we aren't good enough, that we won't make it, that we should just give up.

I think all of us battle with the inner voice of doubt, of fear and of confusion. We all succumb at times to being overwhelmed by life, to being completely weighed down with all that is going on around us, which can leave each of us in a state of turmoil. This was never God's intention for us; our mental health is just as important to Him as our physical health.

We can easily shut down, blocking the voice of God, and letting our own inner voice control our thoughts and emotions.

2 Corinthians 10:5 (NIV) says

'We demolish arguments and every pretension that sets itself up against the knowledge of God, and we take captive every thought to make it obedient to Christ'.

We need to shut down all the negativity that runs rife through our mind and bring it under the authority of God. We need to take hold of the truth and live it in the way we have been called to do.

The battle within our minds is where the devil has his greatest victory, for if he can get us to a place of feeling overwhelmed, or defeated, then he is halfway to getting us to cave or buckle in our strength and our faith.

When we are living in a place of comparison, the inner voice becomes very loud. It tells us that we're not good enough, we'll never be pretty enough, we'll never accomplish as much as someone else, and God would never use us as we're just not that special.

So, what do we do when our inner voice lies to us? Sometimes we believe all that it says, we begin to pretend, or fake it, and in doing so we lose ourselves as we change and become more like someone else, rather than who we were created to be.

Unfortunately, our world of Social Media has changed the way we do life. We no longer live in the moment, enjoying what we have, but we're constantly watching the lives of everyone else, and falling deeper and deeper into the pit of comparison.

You may be a young mum at home with small children, your day could have been going along well, even though it is filled with busyness and mess.

THE INNER VOICE

Somewhere during your day, you find yourself with some down time, so you jump on Instagram to see what's happening out in the world. Suddenly you're faced with seeing a group of your friends all out at the park with their children, everyone looks happy and without a care in the world. The mums are perfectly made up, and looking great in their pre-children jeans, while you're rushing around in your oldest trackpants. Their kids are not covered in vegemite or peanut butter like yours, but are sitting nicely eating fruit and drinking water, not a hair out of place and with smiles that portray happiness and sunshine.

What had started as a good day for you has now turned sour, your inner voice starts whispering to you 'Why didn't they invite you? Maybe they don't like you or your children, maybe they're all talking about you, you don't have what it takes to be part of that group, your kids never look that happy or act that well behaved'.

You've now fallen down the rabbit hole, you've moved from the place of being happy at home with your children, to being discontent with your own life and you're comparing your situation to someone else's.

It's a downward spiral from which there may not be a quick return.

In listening to your inner voice, falling victim to the lies, you've lost your joy, your peace, and your contentment.

This is not the place that God has for you, He has not called you to live your life in comparison, He has called you to enjoy all that He has given you. He is very clear on jealousy and coveting, as He knows that it will only lead to unhappiness and misery.

As a parent we all want to give our children gifts that they will love, gifts that will bring them entertainment and fun. We want them to enjoy what we have given them. Imagine that you have offered your child what you believe to be an amazing gift, but they push it aside in favour of the gift that their friend has just received. As a parent this leaves you feeling disappointed and let down. You had gone to a lot of effort to give your child what you thought was perfect for them, but they would rather have what someone else has.

This must be how God feels when He gives us the life that we have, but we throw it aside as we constantly wish for something different. We keep looking at what our friends have and wish we had that instead.

I would encourage you today to stop listening to the voice inside you that says everyone else is having more fun than you, everyone else is better off than you, and everyone else is loved far more than you.

Let the voice of God be louder than any other voice. Let Him be the one you hear first thing in the morning and last thing at night. Don't fall for the deception of believing everything you hear, listening to what your inner voice is telling you, as it can't always be trusted, sometimes it is easily confused by what it hears, and it will feed you misinformation.

God is the small still whisper, He is the voice you need to hear, the one who speaks truth, who speaks life, and who will lead you on the path you need to follow.

The life you are living may not be perfect, it may not look like the easy and carefree life of your friend, it may not be like those you see on Instagram, or it might not be like the characters of those you read in books, but it's your life, it's real, and it's right for you at this time.

Shut down every negative thought that would rear its ugly head, don't let the devil have a foothold in your thinking. He is not there to help you;

he is there to hinder you. He only has one plan, and that is to destroy you by attacking you in the place that can have the most damage, your mind.

We have been led to believe that there are many different versions of the truth, but as Christians we know there is only one truth, and that is the Word of God. Let Him have the final say in your life, listen to only what He has to say, and allow His voice to be the only truth you hear.

When the devil whispers in your ear, and tries to play havoc in your heart, fight back. Know that he will continue to battle until he wins, therefore you need to take captive every lie that he feeds you, and back it up with God's truth.

You are an overcomer, believe that, and win.

'God is the small still whisper of truth'

21

THE ME I SEE

Over the years when I have looked in the mirror, I have seen very different girls looking back at me. Each girl was a version of me, but at completely different stages in life.

When I was younger, full of confidence, I saw a girl that had the world at her feet, she was pretty, exuberant about life, fun and lived each day as an adventure.

As a young mum I saw a someone who was exhausted, who was running on empty. I saw tired eyes and dull skin; I saw the beginning of lines that were tell-tale signs of worry and stress. I saw a girl who had no idea what she was doing but was going to great lengths to show those around her that she had it all together.

The hardest years of all were those as the mother of teenagers. When that girl looked in the mirror she was overwhelmed, she was tearful, she was full of regret for words spoken or actions taken. She was at a complete loss as to how things had gotten to where they were. This girl in the mirror was someone I didn't really know.

The girl I now see has found her place in the world, is at peace with herself over decisions that were made, knowing that she did her best. She still sees the lines on her face, more than ever before, but knows they are a part of having lived a life filled with every possible emotion. She looks at her body and shakes her head as to how it has changed over the years, and sometimes wishes it looked somewhat better than what it does. But the thing she sees the most when she looks in the mirror is the woman who God has walked with through every season, and the woman He has loved.

All of us see something different when we look in the mirror, we all see the bits of us that we are not happy with, the crooked teeth, the dull and flat hair, the round cheeks, the double chin. There is always going to be faults with what we see, especially when we are comparing ourselves with those around us, it is only natural that we will look at what we have and wish for something different.

I have been blessed with a beautiful daughter. She is a young woman with the world at her feet, and I truly love everything about her. When we have photos together, I look at her youthfulness and suddenly feel old. It doesn't seem like that long ago I was her age, that I had the same glow that she has today, but I have seen many seasons and I am in a very different place to her.

As much as I would love to be her age again, I wouldn't give up my experiences of life for anything. With age has come marriage, children, work opportunities, travel, financial freedom and so much more. I may feel old compared to her when I look at us together, but we are in different stages of life, hers is just beginning and mine is at a place where I am content, and happy. I am where I am meant to be.

For all of us, facing who we are, the stage of life that we are in, can be hard. Things don't always turn out like we think they will. Situations occur and suddenly all that we had known is swept away. The dreams and plans we had for our lives aren't always going to pan out the way we expected. This can be extremely painful, letting go of the life we thought we would have is not easy, or necessarily welcomed.

Looking in the mirror when life deals you hardship can be a startling experience, the woman you see is haggard, she is downtrodden, and she is filled with hurt. Her eyes are no longer filled with joy or peace, but they wear the look of destruction. There is no glow to her skin, but rather it appears to be tired and dull.

This is a hard vision to come to terms with, the girl who you knew and loved is gone, and in her place is a woman who appears to have no bearing on who you thought you would become.

Not every woman who looks in the mirror is happy with what she sees, no matter how beautiful the image is that looks back at her. The woman who wears a heavy heart will never be happy with the face she sees, for that isn't a true portrayal of who she really is. When a heart is filled with trouble and dismay, no amount of makeup can cover the pain of what she feels. Certainly, the people around her will look at her and think to themselves that she has it easy, that her life must be wonderful, but it's all superficial, no one sees what happens when the makeup comes off and real life begins.

Like many of you, I have known seasons in my life where I have looked great on the outside, I have looked well put together, but on the inside, I was a mess. If people could look past what they saw on my face, and could see my heart, they would be shocked. Instead of seeing smiles, happiness, and laughter, they would have seen anguish, tears and pain.

All of us may look beautiful on the outside, but the true mirror, the one that reflects our hearts, can show a very different image.

Proverbs 27:19 (NLT) says
'As a face is reflected in water, so the heart reflects the real person'.

The real us is not the person we see in the mirror, it's not the face, or the hair, but it's what's inside us that counts. It is our heart that is the truth of everything that we are. Our bodies are fleeting, here for but a moment, they change constantly. From the time we are born until we die, we will experience thousands of changes in how we look. We shouldn't judge ourselves or others on the face that is presented to the world, but we should be looking at the heart.

It is in the heart where true beauty lies, it is there that the true us is held. This is the part most people will never see, they will never see the depth of feelings, the joy or the sorrow, the happiness or the pain, the hope or the disappointment.

When we look in the mirror, we see a very made-up version of who we really are, we don't go any deeper, but we only just touch the surface.

When you look at your friends, your colleagues, the other women you do life with, look deeper than what you see on the outside. Just because she's smiling doesn't mean she is happy, just because she brushes off her disappointment doesn't mean she isn't heartbroken, and just because she is well put together doesn't mean her life is the dream she had planned.

We all show the face we want others to see, we portray the version of ourselves that is the most likeable, the easiest to deal with, the one others may like. We don't usually go around with our heart on our sleeve, pouring out to all the many hurts, fears, or worries that we are dealing with.

We keep all the ugly bits to ourselves; we hide away in shame what we don't think we can possibly share with others; we pretend we have it all together because goodness knows what people would think of us if they got to see what our lives were really like.

Today I would encourage you to dig deeper, go below the surface, find the jewel in the crown. See in others what they aren't showing you, look beyond the pretty face in the mirror and see the heart of the women you know.

Walk with them through the hard stuff, let them know it's ok to be real, to be raw and to be the true version of themselves.

Likewise, open yourself up to share who you really are, let your heart be seen, and let others walk with you on your hard days.

It's only in being real with each other that we can find peace in who we are. It's when we allow God to bring trustworthy girls into our lives that we can share our experiences with, that we find the strength to look in the mirror and love the woman we have been created to be.

> *'The real us is not the girl we see in the mirror, but it's who we are deep in our hearts'*

22

OVERLOOKED

Have you ever wondered where God was in that moment when you felt overlooked?

When you were in high school and you missed out on getting picked for the sports team, or you weren't chosen for school captain, or when that boy you liked chose a different girl to be with?

When someone else got the job or the promotion you were going for?

When you desperately wanted a husband, or a baby, or a house, and all-around you friends were getting these things and you seemed to be left behind?

Where was God?

God was where He always is, He was right beside you. He was with you in the disappointment, in the hurt, in the frustration. God never moves away from us; He continues to walk with us. The only people who move away are you and I.

There are moments in life where our pain is real, and very raw. When we look at what someone else has, and think "That should have been me", and in those moments we tend to pull back, we withdraw, and at times we can shut down. We try to fend off the pain, we do this by blocking our emotions, not letting anyone or anything get too close to us, for fear of getting hurt.

We hide behind our disappointment, we put on our fake smiles, and we do our best to carry on like nothing is wrong, when in our hearts we feel hurt and abandoned.

There are times when we feel let down by God.

> 'God why did you give her the job I wanted?'
> 'God why haven't I found a husband; I've been faithful to you?'
> 'God where is my happy ever after?'
> 'God it's not fair'.

This can be the cry of each of our hearts, that life isn't fair because God hasn't given us the one thing we want the most, and yet He has given it to others.

Let me tell you, comparing what you have or don't have, to what others have, will lead you on a very slippery slope downhill. You can never be happy if you're holding God accountable for not providing everything you want, when it appears He is giving all the blessings to someone else instead.

God in His goodness, and His great love towards us, blesses us in abundance, but not necessarily in the way that we think He will, or should. He may not answer our prayers with the response we are looking for, He may make us wait for the very thing we want right now, and sometimes He may just tell us no; not to hurt us, but because He has something else planned that will far exceed what we had hoped or dreamed.

A lesson for each of us is not to limit God by what we think is the best plan for us. Don't look at the girl next door, or your work colleague, or your best friend, and wish you had their life. God's plan for you is unique to you, He has gifted you in ways that are perfectly suited to your personality, and He has set you aside for His purpose.

In the story of Esther, we can see that God had a divine role for her. One that would require discipline, bravery, faith, and trust. Esther didn't just wake up one day and suddenly have all these qualities, these were attributes that God gifted to her over time. She learnt to be the person she was called to be, and therefore was able to move into what God had planned for her. Imagine if Esther spent her whole life wishing she was someone else, if she kept trying to imitate her friends, if she changed her personality to be like someone else, or if she bombarded God with questions about why her life was the way it was when she dreamt of something different. God could never have used Esther if she wasn't attuned to being whom and what He called her to be. She would have missed her purpose. The opportunity to save her people may never have happened if she kept comparing her life to that of someone else and didn't grow in what God had planned for her.

This is no different for you and me.

God has a purpose for each of us, and that purpose isn't the same. You and I will never walk on the exact same path, we will never do the exact same thing. We have different giftings; we come from different backgrounds and have had very different upbringings. Our experiences have shaped us into who we are, and therefore we will never be the same.

The beauty in this is truly spectacular because that is how we have been intentionally created.

If God wanted clones, He could have easily of made them. He could have made millions of identical people, same looks, same responses, same gifts and the same boring lives. However, He chose to make us unique, all in His image, but all different.

Think about that next time you compare yourself to that one person you think has it all, to that girl with the beautiful hair and perfect skin, to that woman with a big family, or lots of money. God made that person in the exact same way He made you, in His image.

When God looks at you, He is abundantly pleased, He doesn't look at your faults, or your downfalls, but rather He smiles, He delights, and He rejoices in you, just as you are. He is not comparing you to someone else, He is not disappointed with the outcome, He doesn't think 'if only'. When He looks at you, He is pleased.

You are, or you are becoming, exactly what God had hoped, dreamt, and planned when He created you. Before you were even a twinkle in the eye of your parents, you were a shining star in the eyes of God. He knew every hair you would have on your head; He knew the exact number of freckles that would adorn your body, He knew your talents and your abilities, God knew you. At no point was He comparing you to someone else, or wishing you were different, or thinking maybe He should try again and see if He got it right next time. At every moment, from conception to birth, and right through to today, God was, and still is, in love with you.

He adores you just the way you are.

God has never overlooked you; He has never given away all the blessings He had planned for you, and you have never walked alone. In those moments when you've felt forgotten, or let down, know that God sees you. He feels your pain, and He carries your disappointment.

In these moments of hurt, remember how much you are loved, how you have been beautifully and wonderfully made, how there is a plan and purpose for your life, and that God has chosen you, and you alone, to do what He is calling you to do.

Let go of the need to follow the crowd, to envy those around you, or to wish for something different, and embrace who you are. Enjoy, and even relish, all your quirky little ways, laugh at your mishaps, and take time to find pleasure in the gifts God has given you.

Be the woman God has fashioned you to be.

'You are a shining star in the eyes of God'

23

EL-ROI – 'THE GOD WHO SEES ME'

THERE ARE SO MANY times in life that we feel passed over, that we don't feel like anyone can see our hurt, or our pain. We feel completely pushed aside, ignored, and left behind. We look around at our friends and our family, and it seems they have been blessed in immeasurable ways, while we are just sitting on the fringe waiting for something great to happen to us.

Let me whisper something deep into your heart, you have not been overlooked, you have never been forgotten and you are certainly not pushed aside. God, the maker of heaven and earth, sees you. Not only does He see you, but He also loves you, He has a plan and a purpose for you, and He considers you a treasure of incredible worth.

I know there are times when all of us feel unseen, we feel disadvantaged, disillusioned and without much hope. We see great things happening to people around us, and we cry out to God wondering when our turn will come, wondering when He is going to bless us in abundance, wondering if things will turn around and life will suddenly get better.

Just because your friend behind the picket fence seems to have it all, don't assume that she necessarily feels that way. She too has moments of wondering if God has forgotten her, of not knowing why her prayers haven't been answered yet, and of feeling completely bewildered by how her life has got to where it is, all of this leaving her frayed at the edges.

One woman in the bible who felt that God may have forgotten her was Sarah. She had an expectation that God would provide a child for her and Abraham, after all, He had promised that Abraham would be the father of many nations, yet month after month she remained barren. Every month she would look around at all the other women in her village, they seemed to have no problem becoming pregnant and producing children, yet she continued to have no child of her own. She worried and fretted over how the promise could be fulfilled if she was not able to give her husband a son. So, Sarah took matters into her own hands, in desperation she gave one of her servants to her husband to sleep with, in the hope that this would produce for him the child she obviously could not. The plan went perfectly, except that Sarah could never have imagined how she would feel when the child that was not her own became her husband's first-born son. Nor could she have imagined how she would feel when Hagar began to act haughty and made her feel less and less like a woman or wife. It made no difference to Sarah that she was the boy's legal mother, she knew in her heart that this child wasn't her own.

Sarah felt that God did not see her, that she was overlooked. She felt that the promise made to Abraham was for him alone, that it was not for them as a couple. Sarah doubted God and allowed her imagination to get the better of her. She became jealous of everything that she did not yet have, and from that, bitterness took over. Instead of waiting for the promise to be fulfilled, she took matters into her own hands, and later regretted the consequences.

We read later in the scriptures, that in the same way that Sarah felt that God couldn't see her and that she would forever live a life that was very different to what she had dreamed of, so too did Hagar.

Hagar was sure God didn't see her, or that He had taken His eyes off her, and was leaving her on her own to deal with the pain, the turmoil, and the distress that she was in. Hagar felt that God had forgotten her, that there was no hope in sight for her or her child. Having become pregnant to her master, and under the spiteful hand of his wife, she had no choice but to make a run for it and headed into the desert. She had no idea how her life or that of her son would turn out. In desperation she prayed to God, and in His goodness, He let her know that He had indeed seen her and would bless her and Ishmael beyond measure.

God, in His infinite goodness and grace, blessed both Hagar and Sarah. In His loving kindness He fulfilled His promise to them both. Neither of these women were neglected, forgotten, lost, or overlooked, but they were both held by Him.

There are many times that we find ourselves in a desert place. A dry barren land that is void of hope, a place where we can't see how the future could possibly be bright or enjoyable. It is a place where we feel God can't possibly penetrate, His hand would never be able to reach down and pull us up from where we lay in dismay.

How wrong we are!

Our God is the one who sees us. He is the one who is with us in the hard times, in the times of disappointment and failings. He sees all that is going on, He doesn't choose what He will or won't look at, but He sees everything, and through it all He is with us.

I know of friends who have wished for things that I have had and feel that God is punishing them because those things haven't happened for them. In the same way I look at some of my friends and think that God obviously loves them more than He loves me, because their blessings seem to be far more abundant, and their lives are more productive and flourishing.

How often do we look at our current circumstances and decide that God has forgotten us? How often do we consider ourselves to be in a hopeless situation and we are sure that things will never get better, that nothing can possibly improve?

We look at our friends who have all the things that we think we should have, the things we think we deserve, or the things we believe God had once told us would be ours, yet we still don't have them, and now we feel so alone.

God has a time for all that takes place, and just as He had a time for Sarah as to when she would give birth to her own son, He has a time for us as to when our own hopes and dreams will be fulfilled. We look at everything through natural eyes, we have expectations with a use-by date, however, God's timing is very rarely like ours. He will not necessarily follow our plans, nor our timing, for what He wants to do in our lives. There will be situations when He will say no to us because He knows the outcome will cause further issues down the track. There will be other instances where

He will say not yet, because we may not be ready for what is to come. Neither of these things mean God doesn't see us, it just means He has a different or better plan.

As parents we sometimes find ourselves in the same situation. We can see what our children want, we can see the pain or distress they are in, yet we can't jump in and give them what they desire, because it will be detrimental for them. Instead, we hold back, we wait until the timing is better, until the situation changes, until they have a bit more maturity to handle what is happening. This doesn't mean that we don't care, or that we don't love them, or that we don't wish that we could change everything for them, of course we do, but sometimes waiting really is the best thing.

Don't look at others around you and feel that they are loved more, or are better taken care of, or that they are of more value. Your situation is different to theirs, and therefore your experience will be too.

God sees you, in every situation, regardless of what you are going through. You are never overlooked, or passed over, and never pushed aside. His eyes are always on you regardless of what is happening or how you may feel.

He is our El-Roi, the God who sees.

'God, the maker of heaven and earth, sees you, you are never overlooked, forgotten or pushed aside'

24

LEADERSHIP

TO ALL MY GORGEOUS friends in leadership, as you well know, you are being watched.

Your life is not your own, and like it or not, what you do is scrutinised.

Every minute of every day other women are looking at you, placing you on a pedestal, and idolising every single thing you do.

The mantle you carry is heavy, it requires great wisdom, much prayer, and a lot of backbone to undergo that kind of revere.

If God has called you into a place of ministry, or to a high-powered career where you wield a great deal of influence, then you are in a position where you can walk with integrity and bring others with you, or you can take a lower stance, and sadly, still bring others with you.

You are the leader on the frontline, you are guiding the troops on the battlefield, you are walking the tightrope and preparing the way for those coming up behind you. This is your opportunity to take the high ground, to ensure that those in your command are well taken care of, that they are well fed, that they are surrounded and protected, and that they are given every opportunity for growth.

With your position comes a great deal of responsibility. It is not easy always being 'on show', of having to stay faithful, be positive, and love during hard times. It can be incredibly difficult putting on a smile when you've been hurt, when disappointment comes, or when you feel overwhelmed. Yet, you will know that as the woman on the stage, the face behind the product, the worship leader, the pastor's wife, the CEO, your role was always going to be one that was watched.

So, how does it feel to be this woman?
How do you cope when your life is always on show?
What do others expect of you, or more importantly, what does God expect of you?

When it's all stripped away, when the curtains close, when the lights go out and the makeup comes off, you, beautiful lady, are still you. You are still the exquisite woman who God lovingly created. You still worship in public, and cry in private. You may still feel bogged down or consumed by doubt. You still look at other women and wonder what it would be like to be them.

At the end of the day, when you are no longer in the spotlight, you are a normal everyday woman with highs and lows just like everyone else.

There are so many women in the bible who were incredible and powerful leaders, women who God raised up to fight armies, to right wrongs, and to rally against the unjust.

One of these women was Deborah, she was a prophet and a judge. She was the epitome of a leader who inspired others, who rallied together a victorious army to win the battle against their oppressors.

She was a woman who showed great courage and faith, she was wise and fair, and in all things, she was obedient to God.

Deborah had everything it took to be a powerful leader. Everyone looked up to her, they listened to what she had to say, they took notice when she gave a command.

God chose this woman to become a mighty warrior for Him, and she served Him well.

If God has called you, if He has raised you up, if He has placed you in a position of authority, then you need to serve Him well. You need to follow in the footsteps of Deborah, being guided by Him in all you do.

In a time of crisis Deborah trusted God, she wasn't leaning on her own understanding of the situation, but she leant on Him for her strength, and to be her guide in every circumstance.

As women we all need good role models to look up to, we need to see how other women are doing life, we need a positive leader to follow. We are looking at those who are on stage leading worship, those who speak from the pulpit, the women leading life groups and the businesswomen succeeding in their roles.

All of us are trying to follow in the footsteps of someone else. We have countless groups we belong to, hundreds of Facebook and Instagram friends that we aspire to be like, as well as the various women we watch on tv. All of us, no matter what our standing in life is, no matter where we are in the pecking order, we are all watching each other.

When God called you into ministry, or into leadership, He did not call you into perfection. He didn't say that you needed to have your life together, or that all you did needed to be top notch. He never had an expectation that you would never fail, or face doubt, or worry about tomorrow. When God called you, His only desire was that you would bring Him your all, and you would serve Him well.

Anything more than that is what you have put on yourself.

As the life of a leader is lived in full view of those around them, it can be easy to think that you need to always be on top, however, your influence can be just as good, and just as strong when you are real, authentic, and raw. When you let others see you walk through hard times and come out the other side, when they see you trust God when life is overwhelming, and when they watch your faith grow whilst you're faced with trials and tribulations.

You don't need to fake your way through difficulties, you don't need to pretend that all is well when it isn't, and you most certainly do not need to make out like God is meeting all your needs when your hands and your heart is empty. That is not serving well, that is just hiding behind a lie.

Living authentically means being real, telling it how it is, being honest about your flaws and your failings. It means leaning into God and trusting Him with the hard stuff, it means walking in faith even when you don't have the answers, and it means sharing your heart, the good, the bad and the ugly.

God wants us to have lives that are lived to our full potential in Him, He wants our stories to inspire others, to give others courage, and to bring glory to Him in all things.

Just because you are a leader doesn't mean that your life is perfect, it doesn't mean that you are living in an ongoing state of perpetual blessing, it doesn't mean that bad things don't happen, unfortunately what it does mean is that you are going through all of that in the public eye.

Your response is what counts, the way you react, what you hold onto, or more importantly, who you hold on to. How you reflect God during times of crisis is the tell-tale sign of the real you. Who you are in public is just as important, if not more so, than who you are in private. The girl who stands before you in the mirror, the one everyone sees, needs to be the girl who has chosen to serve God well.

Not perfect, but well.

Ladies, be prepared for your life of service, for this is what leadership is, it is the calling to serve. To get alongside others, to pray with them, to cry with them, to encourage and strengthen them. It is a call to walk into battle if that is where God has called you. Be prepared for the eyes that will follow you, that may judge you, and that will always be watching you. Be the best that you can be, whilst staying true to yourself, true to the woman who God created.

You may be a leader, but first and foremost, you are a daughter of the King.

> *'In all that you do, in your life of leadership, first and foremost, serve God well'*

25

WOMEN AND HORMONES

THERE ARE TWO MONUMENTAL moments in every girl's life.
The first time she gets her period, and the last time she gets her period. Both of these occasions come with trepidation of what lies ahead.

For the teenage girl stepping into womanhood, it is like crossing into the great unknown. It can be painful, it can bring changes in your body that you haven't experienced before, such as bloating, larger breasts and weight gain, and it can also be a time of unbelievable mood swings.

For the older women it marks the end of an era, a move from being fertile to now being in a completely different season of life. The loss of periods is the highlight, but there is also the sudden menopausal weight gain, the tears, and the feelings of no longer being a complete woman.

Both of these occasions mark a new beginning, and often times we are not always ready for that.

I remember getting my first period, it was awful, I was in agony and was sure that for at least one week, every month, for the rest of my life I was going to be curled up in a fetal position rocking back and forth.

Thankfully it wasn't always that bad, however, I did use the fact that I was female to my full advantage in certain situations. Like when I didn't want to do PE, what male sport teacher is going to argue with the girl holding her stomach and whining on and on about the 'excruciating' pain she is in.

Sometimes being a girl does have its perks.

Of course, as teenage girls we are living in a state of constant comparison, we are always looking to see what the other girls in our class are doing, wearing, or going through.

Most of my friends reached womanhood before me. I was a late bloomer at 13, the last to get my period and the absolute last to develop breasts.

I always remember never feeling like I truly fitted in until I got my first bra. I was far behind all the other girls in the growth area, and whilst they were sporting gorgeous bras in hot pink, fuscia and aquamarine, I had absolutely nothing going on under my school dress. I nagged my mother endlessly about getting a bra, and her comeback was always the same 'that I didn't need it and not to rush into it'. She clearly had no idea that this was all the girls talked about, and I was totally out of the loop.

When we finally did make that all important shopping trip, all I came home with was a crop top, because sadly, nothing else would fit me.

This state of comparison never seems to leave us, we always feel the need to fit in, to be part of the cool group, to not look different to all the other girls. We go to heroic efforts to be the same as everyone else.

However, the girl who is willing to stand out, who doesn't need to be the same, who is willing to walk to the beat of her own drum, she is the girl of great strength, she is the true hero in every story.

Unfortunately, I wasn't that girl, I was just like everyone else, I wanted to be popular, and everyone knew that to be popular you had to fit in with the crowd, so that's exactly what I tried to do.

I think we can all be a bit like that, especially as teenagers, it's such a turbulent time, we are going through so many changes, and all we really want is for others to like us, to see the value in us, and to be seen as normal.

Then in the blink of an eye we reach the other side of our lives. The time when we have done the hard yards, when we have experienced life to the full, when we have grown and changed and become the woman we are today. This should be the part of the story where life is easy, and we are living the dream.

Then, enter menopause.

We are all excited for the day our periods end, thank goodness it's over! However, in its place we are faced with other inconveniences. Firstly, let's start with the weight gain, the days of snacking without consequences are over. A cheese platter and a glass of wine means hours on the treadmill, a donut, cream bun or almond croissant will have you at the gym at 5am and then back again at 5pm. You can forget skimpy bikinis (unless you have been blessed with incredible genes in which case this part of the story is not for you). There is nothing more depressing than that gradual growth around your middle that no amount of dieting or exercise will move. This is the first joy of menopause.

Next comes the mood swings, the elation, the tears, the anger, and for many the complete loss of confidence.

I have been fortunate enough not to suffer too much from up and down emotions, but I know of many friends who have changed from confident, stable women into an absolute hysterical mess, or have gone from being very emotionally well put together to crying at the drop of a hat. A situation that they may have dealt with previously that wasn't really an issue suddenly becomes an insurmountable mountain. They suddenly become overwhelmed, depressed, anxious and fearful. Never underestimate the mood of a women, as it can change in an instant. One minute you will see a beautiful and strong woman, and the next she is falling apart over what appears to be nothing. Hormones can be a wretched and debilitating life changer.

The worst part for many is the hot flushes, this is the most embarrassing part of having reached that stage of life. I had heard that they came at night and it was uncomfortable, but they would eventually pass. Well, I am now in my ninth year of menopause, they don't appear to be passing, and they are not just at night. They are an all-day occurrence, and they come on at the most inconvenient time, like when you are preparing to give a talk in front of people, when you arrive somewhere new for the first time, or when you are out to lunch with friends. And it's not just a little heat or warmth, it's the full blown dipped in a furnace type of heat, complete with beads of sweat, colour changes, the works.

All I can say in answer to all of that is thank you God for doctors and drugs!

Hormones are something all of us girls must deal with. The beginning of our journey as a woman is the preparation time for when we will become mothers. During this time our bodies are changing and are getting ready for what will eventually be their greatest gift to us, the place where our babies will be conceived and grow.

And as we go further on in our lives, our bodies will begin to change, the season of birthing children will end and we will start to see some differences, not all of them will be good, or even welcomed, but they are all a part of womanhood.

The bible doesn't have a lot to say about periods, or about hormones, but it does talk about the sin of Eve leading to pain in childbirth. I think the pain begins long before producing a child and seems to last a long time after. When Eve fell from grace, we see that it is only women who were dished out this punishment, men had other things that they had to deal with, but nothing like what was dealt out to Eve and every generation after her.

So, as you walk through your journey of being of woman, I would encourage you to lavishly love on those around you. Some are doing it harder than you, some don't cope as well, and there are some who will be completely overwhelmed. The emotions that our hormones produce can take us to dark places, can make us imagine things that are not necessarily true, and can cripple us.

Don't compare, don't judge and don't reject, but love the girls in your life.

Get alongside the younger women, from teenagers all the way through, be a role model, be a mentor, and be an advocate for those around you.

God created you, knowing all that you would go through, and His love for you far outweighs anything that you could ever imagine. On your hard hormonal days, cut yourself some slack, knowing that in all things, by God, you are greatly and extravagantly loved.

'The girl who stands out, who doesn't need to be the same, who walks to the beat of her own drum, she is the girl of great strength'

26

THE WORDS WE USE

I DON'T KNOW ABOUT your family, but growing up in our family, it was always drummed into us 'If you don't have anything nice to say, then say nothing at all'.

At the time I thought this was a ridiculous saying, because obviously every time I heard it was when I had something very unkind to say about a person or a situation. If my words weren't pleasing or complimentary it was because of an injustice that was done to me, the behaviour of someone else, or my thoughts on a particular person.

Looking back now, and having spoken the same words to my children, I can see the benefits of this saying.

Our words can be used to wound or to heal, to uplift or to drag down, to encourage or to hurt. Sometimes the words we use can be in jest, they can be a joke, but they can still hurt the person on the other end of the conversation.

Proverbs 15:4 (*NIV*) says

'The soothing tongue is a tree of life, but a perverse tongue crushes the spirit'.

Other words for perverse can be troubling, difficult, unreasonable, obstructive and annoying. Our words have the power to crush the spirit in someone else, to damage them in ways we would never have thought imaginable.

But when we come to someone with words that are soothing, that bring life, that can encourage and strengthen, then we are only going to bring out the best in that person.

Everyone you meet is fighting a battle, it could be small, or it could be all encompassing, you may never know. But how you speak to them could be the difference between them staying strong or breaking down. It could be the difference between them being able to walk with their head held high, or them living in shame.

Words can be more damaging than any other thing you will fight against in your life.

Another saying I grew up hearing from my parents was 'Sticks and stone may break my bones, but words will never hurt me'.

I don't know where in the world this came from, but there is absolutely no truth in this at all.

Words will always hurt, much more than sticks or stones could. The words spoken over us stay with us for far longer than could ever be imagined. I know myself that over the years I have had words said to me that have broken me, left me feeling worthless, have had a profound and debilitating effect on me. The words, although not necessarily said in a spiteful manner, have continued to haunt me, have left me lying awake at night wondering what the person meant, why they would say it or how they could possibly feel that way about me.

Our children will be the first to let us know how they have been wounded by the words we have spoken to them. They will look at various situations in their lives and will see it in a completely different light to us. They will have a perspective that differs from ours and will remember the words we may have used to describe them or their actions.

Just as we have done with our own parents. We will look back on our lives and think over things that were said and done, and we will feel hurt or let down, we may have let the words they spoke wound us or make us feel rejected.

My brother and I grew up in the same house for 23 years until I got married. We lived through all the same situations, yet we have different perspectives on things that happened and how we felt about them.

Your experience will be different to mine, and mine will be different to the girl next door, all of us have had varied life experiences. However, the one thing we all will have had at some point in our lives is hurt. We will have been hurt or shocked at what was said to us, we will be blown away or overwhelmed by the vicious words used by others against us. No one is immune to this, we all come face to face with words of bitterness, hatred, anger, disappointment and disgust.

Think about your own words towards others, the way your insecurities caused you to make fun of someone else, the words you used when you were angry over something that was done to you, or what you said out of fear or confusion.

Every day we speak thousands of words, not all of them are good, or productive or encouraging.

When we are tired or sleep deprived, we tend to be at our worst, we are triggered more easily, we fire up over little things, we jump to conclusions more quickly and tend to overreact.

Our families are usually in the firing line when this happens. We tend to take our moods out on those closest to us. We say things we later regret, we jump in with both feet in our mouth and make a mountain out of a molehill.

The bible talks about being slow to anger, about not firing up, about thinking before we react. There is such incredible wisdom in all of this. Many a friendship or marriage may have been saved if we thought about the words we spoke long before we opened our mouths. If we censored some of what we had to say, if we stopped and prayed before we jumped in with our thoughts and feelings on a situation.

So often we say the first thing that comes to mind, especially when we are angry, or when we are in confrontational situations. We don't like being put on the spot or pressured, we certainly don't like to be attacked, so we bite back. We quite often have not trained ourselves in the art of holding our tongue, giving ourselves and others time and space to think through situations before we set them on fire.

Living with regret is far worse than taking the time needed to think through a situation before responding. In the heat of the moment words are spoken that can't be taken back, there is no undoing the hurt that you may have caused. There could always be the opportunity for apologies and forgiveness, but there is also the very real possibility that this may not happen.

There is the chance that the last words spoken in anger could the very last words spoken at all.

The women in your life, your tribe, the girls you journey with, they are the ones you need to speak to with the sweet and kind words of honey. These are the girls who have your back, who are there for you in the good and bad times, the ones you can cry with, laugh with and do life with.

These women, just like you, are walking on tightropes, they are facing daily battles, and they too are scarred from the words of others. Each of them holds in their hearts the wounds of hurt, of betrayal and of rejection.

Let your words bring them joy, let them bring healing and redemption. Let all that you say to those around you fill them with happiness, encourage them on their journey and remind them that they are loved.

Think too of the words you speak over yourself, sometimes these can be the most damaging conversations of all. The times that you tell yourself that you are hopeless, that you will never be good enough, that you are not loveable. The moments when you put yourself down, or tie yourself in knots with destructive talk, when you tell yourself lies about your worth or your future.

The truth is that the words God speaks over you are life giving. He speaks words of love, of affirmation, of clarity, of forgiveness and of hope. He has a plan and a direction for you, He sees the way ahead and has a purpose in where you are going and what you are doing.

God would never speak to you negatively, or in a derogative manner, He would never choose to hurt you or put you down. He did not create you to criticize you, or to compare you or to callously destroy you, He created you because you are the apple of His eye.

So next time you speak to yourself, do it with this in mind. Know that you are beautiful, you are priceless, and you are chosen. Think of words that agree with that and speak these words over your life.

'Stop and pray before you allow your words to set a situation on fire'

27

OFFENSE

Being offended is something that each of us has dealt with at some point in time. Let's face it, which one of us hasn't been offended? Who hasn't got themselves all worked up and irritated by something that someone else has said, or by a look that they've been given?

Proverbs 19:11 (AMP) says
'Good sense and discretion make a man slow to anger, and it is his honour and glory to overlook a transgression or an offense (without seeking revenge and harbouring resentment)'.

This is a pretty intense scripture, and there is no downplaying it. Good sense makes a man, or a woman, slow to anger, and it is to their honour to overlook an offense. This can be hard, especially as we are instructed to not only overlook the offense, but to not be resentful or seek our own revenge.

This can seem like a lot, and maybe just a little bit hard to swallow. Surely a small amount of resentment is ok? And maybe sometimes it's alright to be angry and hold a grudge?

How many times have you been hurt by things that people have said? Or have felt your hackles rising over the way you have been treated?

It's only natural that you would want to wallow in self-pity, to hold on to that feeling and not want to move forward, not want to forgive and forget. It's so easy to stay stuck in the moment of hurt and disappointment, to hold onto your grudge and nurse it like an oozing wound. This is felt so much more when the offense has been caused by someone we thought was our friend, or by a family member or someone we love.

How could they? Why would they do that to us? What could I have possibly done?

We ask all of these questions and inwardly we feel devastated. Then after the sadness comes anger, how dare they treat us like that, I'll show them.

Next thing you know we are holding on to our offense like a newborn baby, stroking it, comforting it, pacifying it and carrying it with us everywhere we go. We are now fixated on the problem.

I know for myself there have been times when I have been so hurt by what others have done, that I have held on way to hard, and for so much longer than what was really necessary. I have caused myself no end of pain because I refused to let go, I refused to just accept what happened and move forward. I have been fully focused on this one thing and have been unable to just forgive and forget.

The sad thing about this is that the other person had no idea, not a clue that I was harbouring resentment. They might have thought I was a bit off, but they would have no inkling that I was holding the offense so closely that it was now a part of me. They weren't even slightly hindered by what was going on with me, yet I was completely tied up in knots, full of disappointment, anger, and resentment.

I know that during these times I have looked at other women around me and thought to myself how lucky they are, how incredibly blessed they have been to not have experienced what I was going through. I figured that since their lives appeared to be perfect, that they wouldn't have a clue what it was like to feel the way I did.

I watched them with the green eyes of jealousy and thought unkind and uncharitable thoughts about them, I wished that for one minute that they knew what it was like to be walking in my shoes and dealing with what I was dealing with.

I assumed that in their beautiful little bubbles where everything was sunshine and roses that they could not possibly understand what it was like for people to hurt them, to judge them, or to treat them unfairly.

I had placed these women on pedestals that they had no hope of staying on, I had completely misjudged their lives and had wrongly believed that they couldn't possibly understand what it was to go through hard stuff because they lived in such a different world to me.

However, it doesn't matter who you are, what side of the fence you live on, how green your grass is, we all go through things that hurt, wound or offend us. We all find ourselves seething with anger at the injustice of life, and each and every one of us carries a grudge and harbours resentment in our hearts. And for each one of us, it is wrong.

It truly doesn't matter your standing in life, the bible is very clear on this, and it is the same for all of us, we need to use good sense, and we need to learn to let go, to hand over our hurts to God and allow Him to handle them. It's not up to us to seek revenge, to wish for bad things to happen to people, to remain angry or to continue to be resentful.

We are called to love, to forgive, and to turn the other cheek. We are given life changing instructions on how we should respond, on how we should behave, and on how we are to treat others, regardless of what they may have done to us.

If you remember the story of Jesus on the cross, in His final conversation with His Father, He didn't ask God to kill off everyone who was against Him, but rather He said, "Father forgive them for they know not what they do". (Luke 23:34 NIV).

This is incredibly powerful, and such a wonderful example of the life we are to live, the attitude we need to adopt to be more Christ like.

There was no sign of anger or resentment, no offense or retribution, but in His final moments Jesus asks His Father God to simply forgive those who had placed Him on the cross and were about to watch Him breathe His last breath.

He didn't look out at the crowd and wish He was standing in their place; He wasn't angry with how His life was turning out, He wasn't plotting His revenge, He simply and gracefully accepted what was and let go of everything else.

If only we could do the same, if we could let go of the hurt that we feel, and not allow it to turn into a festering sore that moves from deep sadness to all consuming anger. If we could understand that we are not responsible for the behaviour and actions of others, but only for ourselves. If we understood that it is not up to us to fix the problems that others have caused, but rather to not allow them to control us. If we could forgive the person who hurt us, not for their sake, but for ours.

Learning to overlook a transgression rather than building an entire state of defence is a mammoth task, it requires prayer and practise. It is certainly not easy to shake the dust off our feet and keep walking, it's not easy to keep your head held high while the bullets are flying, and it is not easy to remain steadfast in the midst of opposition.

But for our own sake, we need to uphold the biblical principles that we have been taught, for the sake of keeping our hearts clean and for the sake of our mental health. It is absolutely essential that we don't continue to be entrapped by anger, and to allow that anger to make us resentful and hell bent on seeking revenge.

All these feelings lead us down a path of misery, both mentally and physically. They drain us of all our energy, they change our way of thinking, and they destroy our relationships with God and with others.

We need to separate ourselves from the drama caused by other people, shake off the darts that they throw at us and keep moving forward.

Finally, don't think that you are in this boat alone, we have all been there. We all know what it's like to be offended, to feel bruised and battered by the hurtful words or behaviour of others. This is not something only you struggle with, this is for all of us. But for your own sake, use good sense and let it go.

'Use good sense, forgive, forget, and let go'

28

WHO ARE YOU?

Throughout the many stages in a woman's life there is always the question that rolls around in our minds, and that is 'Who am I?'

As a teenager trying to find our place in the world we ask, 'Who am I and where am I going?'

As we reach adulthood, and we are beginning our careers, we are wonder 'Who am I and how do I fit in?'

Then as we get married, and we have children, we see many seasons come and go, yet we are still asking the same question, we are still wondering deep down, 'Who am I?'

There is so much more to that question than could ever be answered with a quick retort. It is not as simple as saying, 'I'm a daughter, I'm a sister, I'm a wife, a mother, a teacher, a nurse, a grandmother, a friend'. The list could go on and on with us giving examples of who we are to the world around us, however, the bigger question is 'Who am I in the core of my being?'

and then secondly, once we try to figure out who we are comes the next big question, 'Who do I want to be?'

The question of who we want to be is far more complex than the one of who we are. We don't necessarily want to be defined by who we are right now, but rather, by who we want to become in the future.

The person you are today is no doubt, very different to the person you were ten years ago. Since that time, you have had many life experiences that have led you to where you currently are, you have walked up and down many mountains and have trudged through some dismal valleys. But each step of the way has led you to the woman you are right now.

In a conversation I had with a friend, we talked about how we may or may not be doing our best. As a busy working mum, time is limited, emotions can run high, and sometimes feelings can be fragile and need to be handled with care. There are so many areas in life that require our attention, and so many distractions along the way.

How do we possibly do our best when we are pulled in every direction?

If I give my best to my workplace, does that mean my family will have to suffer? If I stay up late cooking, cleaning, baking, preparing for the days ahead, does that mean that my work will be impacted the next day because I'm tired?

How do we give our best to God when there is so little time left in the day and He appears to only be getting the leftovers?

Where does that leave us, when there is nothing left in the tank to keep us going?

In all of that, when we feel depleted, and know that we can't possibly be giving our best to everything, we start to wonder who we really are. We start to doubt that we can possibly keep going in this way. We feel ill equipped to handle the task at hand, it's just too much, and who I am just isn't prepared for all that is expected of me.

Who I am, and who I want to be, are not necessarily the same. I want to be the woman who can do it all and do it well. I want to be the employee or co-worker that is respected and trustworthy, I want to be the daughter that honours her parents, I want to be the wife that my husband is proud of, and I want to be the mother that my children will love. Most importantly, I want to be the woman who walks with God, having integrity, offering grace, being faithful in prayer, giving in abundance and loving extravagantly. There is so much that I want to be, but unfortunately, at times, there is so much that I'm not.

When we have honest conversations with the women around us, it seems we are all on the same page with this. When we speak from our heart each of us admits the same thing, so often we fail, we don't give our best, simply because we can't. We are torn between so many obligations that it's hard to know where to start first. So often we have the best intentions for things, we have the greatest of plans, but even the best laid plans go astray. The bible is so true when it says, 'Our spirits are willing, but our flesh is weak' (Matt 26:41 NIV). We may want to get up at 5am in the morning to spend time with God in prayer, but what do we need to sacrifice for that to happen? Will that mean going to bed earlier? Or will it mean we stay up late and not get enough sleep?

This is who we want to be, but it's not necessarily who we are.

Each of us go through seasons in our life where we could have handled certain situations differently. There are times when we say or do things that we are not proud of, and we know that we could have worked harder towards a better outcome. Sometimes the woman that we want to become gets lost, she's stuck somewhere between knowing who she is and still trying to find herself. On the way to becoming a better version of herself, she becomes entangled in circumstances that leave her floundering and unsure what to do.

So, she does what we all do, she does her best. Sometimes this is good enough and sometimes it's just not.

There are days when we look around us and think to ourselves, 'I want to be more like the girl next door'. However, that's not you becoming who you want to be, that's you becoming someone else. Being someone else will never be the right fit for you because that's not how God has created you.

Give some thought to who you have always wanted to be. It may be that you have always wanted to start a small business, so think about what it is you need to do to get you going. Maybe that includes doing some courses, getting some mentoring, speaking to a financial advisor, whatever you think you need to do, today is the day to start that.

Maybe you would like to write a book, start working on that, spend time each day honing your skills, practise with writing 300 words a day, show others what you have written. You will never become who you want to be if you don't make that initial move.

If your aim is to be closer to God, more in tune with Him, then start carving out time each day that you can put aside to spend with Him. Invest in a study bible, set aside a space in your home that you can close the world out and focus solely on prayer, reading and listening to God.

Who you want to be will only become a reality if you invest time in making it happen.

In every season we go through, we may not necessarily know who we are, or where we are going, but God knows who we are, and He knows where He is taking us. He knows that the girl we are today will be ever changing into the woman we will be tomorrow.

Have you ever noticed the beautiful transformation that takes place when the caterpillar becomes a butterfly? It is wrapped up in a woven silk cocoon until the time is just right for it to metamorphis into who it was always created to be.

We too are the same, who we are today, right here and now, is just a steppingstone into who and what we are becoming. Don't worry about the fact that you aren't necessarily the woman you want to be, for God can take all that you are, and in His kindness, and grace, He can transform you into that woman.

Invest time in yourself, find out what you want. Look at your core values and see if they fit with the woman you desire to become. Ask God for His input, that He would show you what it is that He has planned for you, and that He would prepare you for that.

Rather than trying to be like someone else, work on who you are right now, keeping in mind that you were created for a purpose. Once you have found that purpose, step up and become that woman.

> *'Be the woman who walks with God,*
> *with integrity, grace and love'*

29

BE REAL

What is it about us women that make us think we need to be martyrs to our emotions?

We tend to deny all feelings of sadness, tiredness, stress and anxiety and lie not only to those around us, but also to ourselves.

Sometimes, contrary to what you may believe, it's ok not to be ok.

There are times in all our lives where we just don't function at our normal pace. We are battered and bruised, our hopes are dashed, and our emotions are fractured. It is during these times that we could really do with someone in our corner, someone to give us a helping hand and pull us up from the pit we have found ourselves in. However, sadly in true female form, most often the people around us don't even know what we are going through. This isn't necessarily because they aren't our true friends, but because sometimes we do such a good job of hiding who we really are, of shutting down every opportunity for a real conversation, and hiding behind the masks we have made for ourselves. We look good, we perform, we smile, and we tell everyone we're 'good', when deep down we're not.

There is a very fine line between being positive about our circumstance and lying about them. If we are believing God in faith for a good outcome, then putting on a brave face and smiling through despair is a great witness. However, if we are in pain and hurting, and we're shutting everyone out with our pretence of how things really are, then we could be in serious trouble.

Psalm 9:9 (NIV) says
'The Lord is a refuge for the oppressed, a stronghold in times of trouble.'

If you are down and oppressed, if you are in trouble, if you are facing difficulties, and there are things that you don't know how to handle, you are not alone. God is with you in the good times and the bad. He will never give up on you, and you will never be too much for Him. Moreover, because of His great love for us, He has placed us in circles of support. There are other women who care for us, who will surround us, they want the best for us, and they champion us on. However, if we never let them know how things really are in our world, they can't get beside us, pray with us, and help us move forward.

Pretending to be happy when deep down you are struggling is not healthy, and it's most certainly not good for you.
If we are to live authentic lives within our tribe or our community, then we need to let others walk with us, through the good, the bad and in every season of our lives.

We need to show who we really are to those around us, to those that we feel safe with. Most certainly we don't need to tell everything to everyone, that wouldn't be wise, but there are those women in our lives that we can trust, that we can share our hurts and disappointments with, the women who will get alongside of us and help to carry our burden.

True friendship isn't just all the fun stuff that we get to do together, it's not just about shopping and parties, it's not just lunches and spa days, but it's about walking beside each other through the hard times, the not so pretty times. It's about giving and receiving, having a shoulder to ugly cry on, it's sharing our pain when we feel like our heart may break.

Being real is letting go of the unrealistic expectations we have of ourselves, and letting others see who we really are. It's having friends visit when the sink is full of dishes, when the dog has just peed on the carpet, when you are covered in vomit from a sick baby, and when you can't stop the tears caused by a loved one who has let you down.

I once went to visit a friend, and when I arrived at her door she stood with the vacuum in her hand. To me this wasn't a big deal, we could visit, and she could continue with the vacuuming when I left. However, to her this wasn't possible, she couldn't let me into her house in the 'state it was in'.

This is not the sign of a true friendship, it's not real, it's not warts and all.

Our friends should be able to come to our homes and sit amongst the mess, they should be able to pull up a chair at our table, even if it is covered with washing, and have a deep and meaningful conversation with us over a cup of coffee.

And vice versa, we too should be able to do that. We should be able to allow others the privilege of having us call over in our pj's because we couldn't face the thought of getting dressed. We should be able to sob through our story of disappointment, knowing that the one passing the tissues loves us enough to just let us cry.

This is all part of being real with each other.

If you don't have these kinds of friends, get out there and find them.

I know it's not easy just to strike up friendships, but you have to start somewhere. In the heart of every woman is the desire to be known. Make the first move amongst the girls you have in your life, being real with them and giving them the opportunity to be real and known with you.

Of course, there will always be those who judge you, let them and then just move on. These are not the type of friends you need; they may be fun, great to have at a party or social event, but they are not the girls you can do real life with.

Find the girls who are just as real in their stay-at-home clothes as they are in their Friday night drinks clothes, who will drop everything and sit with you in silence when you have no words left to describe how you feel.

Seek out women who laugh hard and cry hard, who have lines on their faces from days of happiness and nights of tears. Women who know what it's like to not have all the answers and have no idea what might come next. Mostly seek out the women who will not only walk with you but will pray with you.

It's the Godly women, those who rely on a higher source, those who know where their true worth is found, these are the women you need in your corner, the women you want beside you through thick and thin, whether you are in the trenches or on the mountaintop, make these women part of your tribe.

There is a time and place in life for a stiff upper lip but having others around you that will allow you to release your troubled spirit is a gift and a blessing.

One of the biggest fears women have in being real with other women is trust. We don't trust that our secrets will be kept, we don't trust that we will still be loved and valued once others see the real us, and we don't trust that the friendship can survive true honesty.

We need to learn to be both trusting and trustworthy. We need our friends to know that whatever they share with us will die with us, we won't be sharing stories with others, we won't be whispering or gossiping, but we will hold to our hearts all that we have heard or seen.

And we need to learn to share with others, maybe starting slowly or with small things, but in order to live authentically, we need to be able to open our hearts and our lives. It's not always easy to do this, but it is the first step in being truthful about who we are and what we are facing.

Live your life in the way that God has called you, in freedom and in love, being real and raw with those around you.

'Seek out friends who will walk with you and pray with you'

30

MOTHERS AND DAUGHTERS

THE RELATIONSHIP BETWEEN A mother and daughter is both precious and precarious. There are so many complex issues involved, so much history, and so many memories. Hopefully for those reading this, the memories will be sweet, tinged with happy smiles and wistful thoughts. But I know that it's not this way for every mother and daughter, there can be so much sadness, or disappointment, feelings of rejection and hurt.

Our relationship with our mother is our first step into the world of friendship. How we have been treated by the first woman in our lives will play a big part in how we see ourselves, the world around us, and the other women in our village. The love we may or may not have received from our mums will dictate how we go about building relationships with the girls we go to school with, those we meet at work or church, and those we make a part of our own families, sisters not by blood, but by choice.

Both my own mother and my daughter are incredibly strong women. They can be feisty, they hold firm to their beliefs, they have minds of their own and opinions on every subject under the sun. Between the three of us, three generations of women in one family, we are all fiercely independent, full of self-confidence, and committed to what we believe to be right and true.

I have been truly blessed to have both these women in my life, one who raised me, and the other who I have raised. Each of us shares a strong bond of love that is incredibly precious.

I know that how we raise our daughters will ultimately play a very large part in the women they become. What we teach them when they are young will stay with them, as will the words we speak over them, and the character traits we model for them, these will all help to define their future belief system.

My daughter is undoubtedly one of the strongest young women I know. She has never been one to be easily swayed by friends, or to feel the need to fit in with the crowd. Whilst as a teenager I was always concerned that I wouldn't be part of the cool group, I always did my best to teach her that she didn't need to be part of any group, she just needed to be herself and that would attract others to her, and it has.

Our daughters are watching us, they are listening to how we speak, both to ourselves and to others, they are weighing up if our value system is right for them. These young impressionable girls are wanting to see what they need to do to cope in a world full of chaos, full of anxiety, and full of dysfunction.

One of the best things we can do for our daughters, our nieces, and our granddaughters, is to live authentic lives. To be who we really are, to live the truth of what God has called us to. We need to be honest and real and raw. We need to let them see that sometimes life can be hard, but God is still faithful. We need to show them that it's ok not to always have everything together, but to trust that God will work all things together for good.

Our girls, the next generation, those incredible women who are coming up behind us need to know that success isn't built on what we have, but rather on who we are. That morals and values are far more important than fame and fortune, and that we don't need to strive to be someone else, for who we are is more than enough.

A godly mother, one who prays for her children, who encourages them, who walks with them in every season, is the one who will impact her child for good. She is the one they will turn to when things are hard, when they need to know what to do, when they are searching for biblical perspective and when they are in need of prayer.

How you relate to other women will have a huge impact on how your daughter relates to others also. If you are filled with jealousy about what your friends have that you don't, then it's most likely that your daughter will follow in this way. If you always see the negative in your friendships, then so may she, and if you find yourself living in a state of offence, then it's more than likely that your child will always have that as her default too.

We may not realise that they are watching us, but they are. They see how we relate, how we react, and how we respond. They pick up on all the little tell-tale signs, the poor attitude, the tears, and the bickering or nit-picking. From the time our girls are small they are looking to us, seeing how we behave, and ultimately, they are following our lead.

We need to be showing a good example. I know this isn't always easy, sometimes we lose our heads, we are faced with disappointment, we are overwhelmed by life. But as much as we can, we need to show our girls how to live their best lives.

We all have memories of growing up that can be both good and bad. There will be things that you have held onto that have been hurtful, and in some cases have wounded you so deeply that you're not able to function as well as you should. There will be things that you will remember that have hugely impacted who you have become, that have changed you in ways that are both positive and negative.

One thing I would like you to think through, and this could be hard, but your mum did the best that she could. It may not have been what you thought she should do, or what you yourself would do, but she did the best she could at the time.

I know this can sometimes be difficult to believe, you look back at situations and you feel broken and let down, you doubt that she loved you, and you are horrified by the choices she made. However, you don't always know the full story, you don't know why she did what she did, the state of her mind, the full situation or what else may have been going on at the time. Whatever it was that happened, that left you feeling alone, or lost, or unloved, it's time to let it go. Let God deal with how you feel, with the aftermath, and the repercussions, and move on.

As women, we can all hurt each other. Sometimes we do it knowingly, and other times it's just an unfortunate thing that happens. We bite back, we retaliate, we use our words as weapons. We all have something within us that snaps, and we decide that enough is enough, we're going to take matters into our own hands and change the situation that we find ourselves in.

Some food for thought for you, God is the only one who can seek revenge, who can fight on our behalf, who can go into battle for us. We need not seek our own justice, for He will do it for us. It would never be

His intention that we would go up against another daughter of His in anger, that we would choose to raise up an army against another woman of God, or that we would backstab and slander her. He would never want us to turn others against her, or to put ourselves above her in all things. This is not the ideal behaviour for a Christian woman.

If you have found yourself as a mother behaving like this, it's time to stop. Don't let the little girl you are raising see this as the norm, don't let her think it's ok to be hurtful or spiteful to other women.

Teach your daughter to love, to forgive, to uplift and pray for those around her. Teach her to turn the other cheek, to forgive easily and not harbour a grudge. Teach her to encourage others, to include them, and to walk beside those who are struggling.

As mothers we need to be leading by example, teaching from a young age, and following that through to the time of maturity.

In your role as a daughter, a mother, or a grandmother, you have so much to impart to those coming behind you. No matter what your age, you have wisdom to share with others. You have life experience that you can draw on that will help other girls and women to reach their full potential. Your position is one of power, because you are in the place of being able to live your life in a real and tangible way, to show others the way forward, and ultimately, to let the girls and women in your tribe see the hope of Christ in you.

> *'The best thing we can do is to live authentic lives, to be honest, real and raw'*

31

DECISIONS

So many of the decisions we make in life are based on what we see, what we feel and what we think. We see others around us living a certain way, and we decide that we should follow in their shoes and try to emulate them. We feel like our lives are sub-standard whilst theirs appear exciting and fun, so we make choices that will hopefully give us the same outcome that theirs have. We think that everyone around us is in a better place than us, so we base all our decisions on how we can get to the same place as everyone else.

This thought pattern completely rules out the plans that God has specifically for us. It totally negates His desires for us, His giftings in us, and His promises towards us. It strips us of who we are, as we try to be a carbon copy of someone else. It hinders all that we have within us, our genetic makeup, our talents, and our unique calling, as we become something or someone we were never meant to be.

Isaiah 55:9 (NIV) says

'As the heavens are higher than the earth, so are my ways higher than your ways, and my thoughts than your thoughts'.

God's ways, His thoughts, His purposes, and His plans are far higher than ours. He can see the beginning from the end, and He knows what the future will look like. God will have a far greater end game than we could ever imagine.

As a teenager I wanted what everyone else had. If my friend was going to buy the latest outfit, then I absolutely had to do that too. If they decided to enrol in extra-curricular study, I suddenly thought I might as well jump on that band wagon. If they were going to a party on Saturday night, then there was no way that I could miss out on that opportunity. All my decisions, like most teenage girls, were directed by what my friends were doing. Peer group pressure at its finest.

As I got older that didn't necessarily change, sure the choices that I made were different, but I was still heavily influenced by what everyone else was doing. If I looked over the fence long enough, I was sure that the grass in my friend's yard was getting greener and growing longer by the day.

Many women make decisions based on other women. This is one of the main reasons why fashion and home magazines sell in their millions, because we are all watching to see what is being worn, or being done by others, so that we too can do the same. We try to copy what we see, thinking that will make us happier, or somehow more likeable. Many women will buy things they can't afford, wear things that don't suit them, or carve out lives that are not true to who they are because they want to fit in, be seen as popular or look like they are living the dream.

I grew up in the days of Young Talent Time, oh how I loved that show, and although I absolutely can not sing to save myself, I always pictured myself as Tina Arena or Karen Knowles. I was convinced that once I got noticed, once people heard my angelic voice, then my life was suddenly going to change overnight. I would be a massive success, I wouldn't need to go to school anymore, who needs classrooms when I would be a household name. I was glued to the television on Saturday nights, singing along into my hairbrush, and wondering what I could possibly do to find my way into the ever-popular Johnny Young Talent School.

Sadly, I never made it, no amount of wishing or dreaming was actually going to replace the fact that I had no musical talent, and that simply making the decision to be the next voice of Australia was never going to get me there. That was simply not my calling.

Have you ever made a decision that was based purely on watching someone else? Have you ever thought to yourself that if you just 'tried' to be like them, then maybe you could pull it off and you could follow in their footsteps?

The funny thing is, if God had wanted us to be just like someone else, He would have made us that way. If He had wanted two Tina Arena's, He could have given her a twin, but He didn't. He made Tina exactly as she is, and He made me exactly who I am. Sure, there are plenty of things that I can do to improve who I am, but there's nothing I should do to necessarily change the core of who I am.

God wants to change us from the inside out, He wants to grow us in our gifts and talents. He wants us to use all that He has given us for His glory, but He also wants us to stay true to who we are. He doesn't want us to eradicate all that He has made us to be so that we can be just like someone else.

At the time of our conception, He had already formed the women we would be, He had already planned our days, He had already structured our beings and He had lovingly crafted us into all that He had planned and purposed for us.

God did not choose to give me an amazing singing voice, but He did give me a way with words. He didn't give me long legs like a gazelle, but He did give me a body that was able to carry children. He didn't give me all the money in the world to do with as I pleased, but He gave me blessings enough that I would be able to live a comfortable life and share with others.

Sometimes the decisions that we make are based on our selfish desires, they are based on all that we want rather than on what we need. We make decisions that can sometimes be detrimental to us as they are formed whilst coveting what others have.

The best decisions we make are the ones that we invite God into. The ones where we seek His approval, we ask for His blessing, and we acknowledge His will.

God's plans for us are always for our good. They are always based on what He knows about us, what He loves about us, and what He desires for each of us. He would never do anything that would hurt us or would leave us floundering. He always has our best interests at heart and would go to the ends of the earth to keep us within His perfect will.

Yet God will never make decisions for us, He will always allow us to make our own choices, He will always give us space to think for ourselves, and therefore to form our own opinions on things. God will guide us, He will show us better options, He will open and close doors for us, but ultimately the final decision is always ours.

We need to base our decisions not on what others think, but on what God thinks. Our friends and family can't possibly see what lies ahead for us, they can't see the outcome of our choices, they can never know how things will work, that is for God alone.

God sees and He knows when we are basing our decisions on what we see others doing, He knows that what will work for our friends will not necessarily work for us. He knows the choice we make today to buy a bigger house, because that's what our friends have done, will impact us in far greater ways than we could imagine. He knows that spending money we don't have on holidays, just because our neighbour has, will have an adverse outcome for us. He knows that spoiling our children so that they feel as loved as the children next door, will only cause us further grief down the track.

God is all knowing about all things. We may try to justify our actions, we might pretend that we have a spiritual reason behind all that we do, but God can see into our hearts and into our minds and He knows the truth.

Our decisions can be life changing, they can be the difference between living a good life and living a great life. They can profoundly influence our future and lead us down a path that was never intended for us.

Our decisions need to be God led, not people led. They need to be based on His direction for our lives, not on following a whim, or being swayed by the next best thing.

The greatest gift we can give ourselves, both for today and for tomorrow, is to ask God to lead us in all that we do, to bring all our thoughts, choices, and decisions to Him, and to allow Him to direct our path.

*'God wants to change us from the inside out,
He wants to grow us in our gifts and talents'*

32

SOCIAL MEDIA

THE AREA OF SOCIAL media can be a very hard one to address. There are many varying opinions as to whether it is good for us, whether it helps us to connect with others, or whether it is the detriment of us all.

I personally enjoy Facebook and Instagram. I enjoy scrolling through and seeing what others are doing, or keeping up with family overseas, or even following the myriad of pet pages that I can't seem to resist.

However, I am not in a place of believing everything I see, nor do I presume for one minute that every happy photo I see is the outworking of a perfect life. I know that we all post the photos we want others to see, we post the holiday snaps, the family looking their perfect best, the days out, and our homes looking pristine and beautifully presented.

This is not real life; this is just the slideshow we have for others to see.

Social Media is a place for us to show off, it's a place where we escape from our mediocre lives and show the world just how great it is to be us. It's the place where we flaunt our bikini bodies, new hairstyles, amazing love life, flashy cars, and adorable children.

What it's not is the place where you see failed marriages, prodigal children, broken hearts, debt induced depression, anxiety, or alcoholism. We don't tend to air our dirty laundry, we don't show our ugly bits, and we most certainly don't let anyone see our broken and failing lives.

Social media is the perfect place for us to lie about who we really are.

For the woman who is suffering, both Facebook and Instagram are her greatest enemies and biggest downfall. It is the place where she will feel at her worst, where her every failure will be brought to the forefront of her mind, and where she will feel like she is missing out on all that life has for her.

It is here that she will see that the grass appears to be greener on the other side of the fence, and she will lose all contentment in life. She will look at the lives of every other woman she knows and suddenly her existence will pale in comparison.

If this is you, it's time to stop watching the lives of others. It's time to realise that what you see online is just a snippet of someone's life, it's not the full picture. It may be a ten-minute burst of joy amid a devastating situation, it could be a few photos of a family holiday that looks amazing but was fraught with tension, it could be a smile that is really just covering the tears that have only just stopped.

I know through the many lockdowns that came with Covid19, I would watch for photos of my family and friend's interstate and overseas. I would see places that weren't affected by isolation, rising numbers, sickness, and months of being held as prisoners in our own homes. I would look at what others were doing, and I would be racked with jealousy. I would wish I could be anywhere other than where I was. I would feel ripped off as I saw people out and about enjoying life while my family and I were spending day after day stuck at home, while in other places of the country or world, people were living a very different experience.

In these instances, spending time scrolling was not good for me. It took my eyes off the fact that I was at home, where I was being kept safe, and it had me coveting everything that I didn't have, the things I couldn't do or the places I couldn't go.

Social Media can be the detriment of all of us if we believe it to be absolute truth, if we see it as portraying the real and everyday life of those around us.

Except for the very rich and famous, there are few of us who are parading around on beaches 24/7. Not too many of us are sailing the Whitsundays on a regular basis, nor are we drinking cocktails overlooking an endless lagoon pool.

All of this is just a blink of the eye, it's a momentary escape, and it's not the regular lifestyle that our friends are living.

If you see your friends doing this, be happy for them, this is their annual holiday. It's the dream they have worked hard for, it's the five or ten days out of the year where they get to go off and enjoy the fruits of their labour. Let them post their happy snaps, like them, comment on them, and then move on.

This is no more their normal life than it would be yours. Don't be jealous of what others are doing, don't focus on all that they have that you don't. Just because it isn't your time for this now, doesn't mean it won't be in the future. And when that time comes, it will be you posting the amazing photos, and it will be your friends liking, commenting, and wishing they were you.

A few years ago, we had some new friends from church come to lunch. During that time, we happened to show them our photo album of a family holiday we had recently had. Of course, like all family photos, we all looked happy, like we were having the best time, and that we enjoyed every moment of our week together.

Unbeknown to me at the time, the woman had gone home in tears. She had looked at our photos and had struggled with the fact that our family seemed so happy, when her own was not. She had seen what appeared to be the perfect family and it had left her feeling disgruntled and gutted over how her own family looked.

I was devastated that she felt this way, I wish I could have told her what it cost to get some of those photos. I wish she knew about the arguments, the backbiting, the tears, the frustration, the anger, and annoyance. I wish I could have told her that our family is not perfect, I wish she could have known the brokenness in my own heart over things that were happening in my family. But the opportunity had passed and there was nothing I could say that would take back or fix how she felt in that moment.

This too is what it's like when we scroll Facebook and Instagram. We see what others choose to let us see, we don't see the backstory. We see the victory photos, we see the end result, we see the finish line, trophy, and all.

Don't be fooled into thinking that what you see is the way it is. Most things are very seldom what they look like. There is always more to a picture than what you see.

Deuteronomy 5:21 (MSG) says

'No coveting your neighbours' wife (or husband in the case of us women), no lusting for their house, field, servant, maid, ox, or donkey either – nothing that belongs to your neighbour'.

I very much doubt in today's day and age that any of us are coveting our neighbour's ox or their donkey, but I certainly wouldn't mind borrowing their maid, and I do have some amazing homes around me that I would move into in a heartbeat.

But we are told not to covet what someone else has, and that includes watching others online and wishing we were them or that we could live like them.

If your friends appear to be living the dream, thank God for blessing them, if they appear to have happy and fulfilling lives, or they have had many great successes, cheer them on. Don't wish for what someone else has, you don't know what it cost them to get where they are, you don't know what they may have suffered or what they are currently walking through.

Take your focus off all the things that others have that you may not and be grateful for what you do have.

I would say to all of us posting online, think of others before uploading a photo, think of how it appears, think of the hurt it could cause, think about the anxieties it could produce. There is absolutely nothing wrong with sharing your life through social media, but just be aware of the reaction it can cause in those who may not be doing so well, for those who are at the end of their rope, for those who may feel broken.

And for those of you scrolling through, remember that this is just a snippet of someone's life, it's not the full story, it's just a small part of a bigger picture.

If you find that it becomes overwhelming, or that you are obsessing over what everyone else is doing, it's time to stop.

Stop following others, stop subscribing, stop liking, and maybe just take a break.

Live your own life in the here and now, enjoy the simple things and be fully present to those around you.

Living through social media is not living at all, start living and loving the life that God has blessed you with, and leave everything else behind.

'Social Media is a place to show off, it's not reality. Don't believe everything you see'

33

SOCIAL STANDING

BELIEVE IT OR NOT, you are more than just where you stand on the social ladder.

You are not your job, or your financial status, or your business, or your family name.

You are so much more than all these things. This is not your identity; it is not who you are.

You are a woman of quality, a daughter of the king, a chosen vessel, and a light in dark places.

It doesn't matter what family you were born into, how much money you have, the career you have chosen, or whether you have the right 'look', this is not the essence of who you are, for you were destined for so much more than this.

How often do we look at other women and we're pulled in by how they look, the homes they live in, the cars they drive, or what they do for a living? We get blind-sided by their designer clothes and their perfectly put together family.

What we overlook is seeing the real women behind the façade, we don't see the struggle she has to keep it all together, we don't see the lonely days and the silent tears, we don't see the sacrifices or the heavy hearts.

Our modern-day world may have given us so much more than our mothers and grandmothers had, but it hasn't necessarily made for a better life. We can make it look all nice and shiny on the outside, but on the inside we are all still the same, we are all wanting something different, we are all wanting an intimate connection with others.

There is no greater story in the bible about comparison, jealousy, and rivalry than that of Joseph and his brothers.

Joseph was highly favoured by both God and by his father. He was the favourite son, he received a beautiful coloured coat by his natural father, and from His spiritual father he was given the ability to dream prophetic dreams.

All of this infuriated his brothers, they grew to hate him for the things he possessed that they didn't. The despised what they considered his lofty ways, for thinking he was better than them, and for this they plotted ways to get rid of him.

Nothing much has changed in the thousands of years since this story was written. Brothers and sisters, whether physical or spiritual, are still jealous of each other. They still compare their lives to that of others and find themselves deeply longing for something more. They look at the gifts that others have been blessed with and they wish they had them, they want some of the glory that others seem to be basking in, and so comes the rivalry.

It may not come in the form of throwing the other person in a ditch, at least not in the true sense of the word, but there are certainly many other ways to destroy a life or a reputation, and sadly women and men the world over, have become experts at it.

God never designed us for this kind of life. It was His intention that we would live together in unity, that we would walk side by side in a loving relationship with each other and with Him. However, that ideal was destroyed when one woman decided she wanted what she knew she couldn't have, and ever since that day, we have all followed in her footsteps.

Each of us is filled with longing and desires. There are things we wish we had, and situations we wish were different. Not everything we want or hope for is detrimental, there is nothing wrong with having goals or dreams that we are working towards, as long as we know that the end game will not change who we are.

If you are working towards a high-flying career, well done to you. I'm sure there have been many years of study, of giving up your free time, of making sacrifices, nothing will have come easy. But when you reach that place where you can celebrate what you have achieved, deep down, you are still you. Certainly, some things will have changed, but the core of who you are, what you stand for, what you believe in, it's all the same. Your career doesn't change the person you are, the heart of you as a woman.

I have a gorgeous friend who was living the so-called dream. A beautiful home, a large loving family, a nice flashy car, and a fantastic business. However, through no fault of her own she lost all of it. She went from having great social standing, a place in the community, to suddenly having nothing. The friends she thought she had were nowhere to be seen, the invites stopped coming her way, the bank wanted what little she had left, and soon she was left with very little at all.

Through all of this, what remained was her tenacity, her strength of character, her fighting spirit, and her incredible ability to hold her head high. She was not going to be crushed by all that she lost, no matter how painful it was, but she was going to continue to live her life despite what was happening to her.

We need to know that we are more than what we hold in our hands, for what we have today could be gone tomorrow. The things we have, that we consider so important and precious are not who we are. It doesn't matter if your name is up in lights, if your bank account is flourishing or if you look good to those around you, what matters is who you are on the inside.

It is our core being, our belief system, our heart and soul that really makes a difference. That is what will hold us in good stead if the ground beneath us should shift. It is these things that we need to hold dear.

Our relationship with God and with others should be the focus of what those around us see when they look at us. They shouldn't be interested in what material possessions we have, the title we hold, or who we do or don't know. It should be whether we love Jesus, whether we serve Him, whether we are kind and considerate to those we meet. They should see in us an example of servanthood, a loving heart and a spirit that is full.

Our social standing should be based not on what we have, but on who we are. Who we are when we are in the supermarket waiting our turn, when we are stuck in traffic on a busy day, when we have been wrongfully accused of things that we have never done. It is then that who we really are comes to the forefront, when our character is on show, when we crack under pressure, when our façade fails us, and we show the world who we are at the core of our being.

The same applies when we look at others, we shouldn't be impressed by looks, material possessions, or ladder climbing. None of this should mean anything to us. We shouldn't be jealous of all that others have that we wish was ours.

What should impress us is godly character, faith, leadership abilities, love, and grace. It is the heart of God in others that should move us, this should be our reason for trying to emulate those around us. It should be what drives us to be better women.

There is nothing behind our neighbour's picket fence that is better than anything we already have, they don't have some magic potion for a perfect life, they don't come out of battles unscathed or unscarred. They have problems in their family just like we do, they have their own skeletons in the closest, they too have issues that they are dealing with.

Your friends, your neighbours, your sisters, and your colleagues, they are all on a journey that goes over mountains and through valleys, their path is just as bumpy as yours. They might not be experiencing the same things as you, but they too have moments when their world is turned upside down and they are left feeling shattered and hurt.

So, before you look over the fence and see how green the grass is, look around you at all that God has blessed you with. See your glass half full, look through your rose-coloured glasses, and don't buy into the lies that the enemy would have you believe.

Remember, that to others, you may be living behind the picket fence, it's all just perception.

No matter where you are on your journey, God is there with you. Enjoy each day, and give thanks to Him for all that you have, all that He has given you.

For all that you are is a testament to all that He is.

> *'We are more than what we hold in our hands,*
> *for it could be here today and gone tomorrow'*

34

DISNEY PRINCESSES

As little girls most of us grew up reading and dreaming about living the life of a Princess. The infamous Walt Disney, created an empire built on beautiful young women who wore incredible dresses, lived in castles, and married their Prince Charming. There have been movies made, dolls sold, and musicals performed on the life and times of these Princesses.

It isn't until we grow up that we realise that the life of a Disney princess wasn't as great as we had always thought. They didn't always grow up in happy homes, they weren't always parading around in ballgowns, and they certainly didn't have lives that were carefree and easy. Before some of these girls got their happily ever after, they had to suffer and endure some very hard situations.

My favourite story growing up was that of Snow White, I had loved that she got to live out in the country side with lots of little guys who loved her, she was friends with all the animals in the forest and eventually she is saved by the kiss of a prince who falls madly in love with her. Somehow in reading that fairytale, I only focused on the positive aspects, yet there was so much more to the story than the happy ever after.

Snow White grew up in a home without her mother, and she had to endure the hardships that came when her father married a woman who was filled with jealousy towards her. This evil woman went so far as to seek out someone that would kill and get rid of her once and for all. This is certainly taking the issue of comparison to a whole new level, to be so consumed with the looks of someone else that you will go so far as to have them destroyed, so that you can be known as the most beautiful woman in the land. As adults, when we read through this story in its entirety, the picture it paints is very different to what we might of read as a child. We start to see the background more clearly and realise that in order for Snow White to get to the part in her life where everything works out well, where she becomes a princess, the girl she was always destined to be, she first has to go through some hard experiences and some very troubling times.

Another Disney story that is filled with heartbreak is that of Cinderella. She too lost her mother at a very young age, and although she had a father who loved her, once he remarried, life as she knew it began to change. Not only was there a new woman in the house, but she had brought with her, her own two daughters, girls who spent all their time bickering, and had no care or kind feelings towards their new stepsister. Unfortunately for Cinderella, the lady of the house was a bitter woman, and once her new husband, Cinderella's father, passed away, leaving her with no means to enjoy the life she had entered, she became fueled by anger. She blamed everything on Cinderella and decided that her stepdaughter would have to become the servant to her and her own daughters. Poor Cinderella was moved out of her bedroom and put in the attic, where her days were spent with the rodents who ran through there. She was treated terribly, scoffed at, scorned and hidden away.

We can see in reading this, that Cinderella wasn't just a princess who married a prince. She was a girl who lived a hard life, she was starved of love and affection, she was rejected, she was treated badly, and her life was terribly unfair. In order to get her happy ever after she had to endure the sadder side of life, and to walk through many times of hurt and disappointment.

Each of us could relate to the life of a Disney princess, we can all agree that life can be hard, and also very different to what we had expected. Sadly, things happen that are out of our control. The choices or behaviour of others can leave us damaged, can put us in danger, and can threated to ruin the rest of our lives. We can start out with the best of everything, but through no choice of our own, things can suddenly change. People we love leave, circumstances become difficult, and life as we know it can be turned upside down.

We can see that in these stories, both girls suffered at the hands of other women. We see that jealousy and fear was the driving force behind the behaviour, and that the hurt caused came from a bitter and hardened heart. Both girls felt very alone and suffered terrible rejection. They were subject to abuse and hatred and made to feel that their lives were of no value.

I know that there are many women who will identify with these stories. They will feel their heart skip a beat as the memories of hurt come to the surface. They know the pain of being rejected, of being pushed aside, and of being the subject of jealousy and hate. It is a story they are all too familiar with, and it reminds them of a time in their life that they would rather forget.

However, in all good Disney movies, there is always a happy ending, the girl always gets her man and together they ride off into the sunset. Although this is not always the case in real life, we do find that the ebb and flow of life ensures that our situation can, and usually does turn around. Things do get better and the hardships that we thought would last forever eventually end and we are able to move forward. We may not marry our prince, but we can move out of the grips of those who seek to hurt or destroy us, and we can forge a new life for ourselves. It may look different to what we had thought it would, it may not include a castle or ballgowns, but it can be beautiful just the same.

It is interesting that when we read these stories, the young girls who leave behind their wretched lives and become princesses, don't appear to harbour a grudge. They aren't filled with bitterness over what happened to them, or towards those who hurt them. They manage to go forward, and step into their new lives, leaving behind all that could have so easily destroyed them. We see them rule their kingdoms, alongside their husbands, with the upmost kindness.

The life of a princess is one of servanthood, although she is far above all of those around her, it is her calling to serve her people and her country. Both of these young girls were well taught in how to serve others. Although they learnt this under very difficult circumstances, and not through any choice of their own, they were both trained in how to wait on, care for, and sacrifice their all for the good of someone else.

There is so much that we as women can glean from the life of a Disney princess, we can see that our journey isn't always going to be what we think it will be, and that not everyone is going to be on our side or see us as we were created to be. We can learn how to be content and joyful in our current circumstances, even if they aren't what we hoped for, and we can find the good in everything. We can walk away from painful situations without having hate in our hearts, and without seeking retribution. We can forgive and move forward, still being able to show kindness and love to those around us.

All the attributes that these young girls showed, are the characteristics and traits of a godly woman. They are the benchmark of a life well lived, and they are the outward working of Christ in us. We can see that through all of the experiences that each girl faced, in the end she still chose to love. She still had a clean and pure heart and a beautiful spirit.

No matter what you may have gone through, what life has dealt you so far, or where you are on your journey, don't let it destroy you. Choose to be the bigger person, to let your life be a beacon of light, and to continue to love without ceasing. Let go of all that which has hurt you and fulfill your calling with purpose. Don't look back on all that you have suffered through and wish that things were different but decide today that this is where you will draw your line in the sand, knowing that this is your new beginning.

You may not be part of a Disney story, but you are a princess in your own right, for you my friend, are a daughter of the King.

*'Let go of all that which has hurt you,
and fulfill your calling with purpose'*

It has been so hard to know where to finish this book, I could go on and on writing about all the 'stuff' that us women experience. We are incredibly unique, very diverse and sometimes overly complicated.

But the one thing that I want you to know, is that regardless of what age you are, how you are wired, where you stand in life, or what you struggle with, you are deeply and immensely loved.

God handpicked you before the beginning of time, He specifically chose you and has set you apart. You are not just one of the crowd, you are not overlooked, and you are not forgotten. You have been fearfully and wonderfully made, and He takes great pleasure in you.

Don't ever underestimate your value, don't wish you were someone else, and don't keep looking behind the picket fence of all those in your street wishing for something different. Believe the truth about who God says you are and walk forward into all that He has for you.

Always remember, you are a much loved, highly valued, daughter of the King.

Love Dawn

www.ingramcontent.com/pod-product-compliance
Lightning Source LLC
Chambersburg PA
CBHW060527100426
42743CB00009B/1456